THE BIRTH ORDER EFFECT

How to Better Understand Yourself and Others

CLIFF ISAACSON AND KRIS RADISH

Adams Media Corporation
Avon, Massachusetts

Published by
Adams Media Corporation
57 Littlefield Street, Avon, MA 02322 U.S.A.
www.adamsmedia.com

ISBN: 1-58062-551-7

Printed in Canada.

J I H G F E D C B A

Isaacson, Clifford E.
    The birth order personality method : how to better
understand yourself and others / Cliff Isaacson and Kris Radish.
        p.   cm.
    Includes index.
    ISBN 1-58062-551-7
    1. Birth order. I. Radish, Kris. II. Title.
BF723.B5 .I73 2002
155.9'24—dc21   2001055204

*This book is available at quantity discounts for bulk purchases.
For information, call 1-800-872-5627.*

Contents

Authors' Note

While many of us are familiar with the ins and outs of birth order, *The Birth Order Effect* is a new and exciting way to understand who we are.

The Birth Order Effect is about Birth Order Personality. This is totally different from a person's chronological birth order. For example, a first-born will always be a chronological first-born. That is not necessarily true of his or her Birth Order Personality.

To keep these two classifications separate, chronological birth order will be referred to in *The Birth Order Effect* using lowercase letters. Thus, a reference to a "first-born" would pertain to the oldest child in a family, while a reference to a "First Born" would relate to someone who has this particular Birth Order Personality.

Establishing these distinctions now will help you as you begin this journey toward understanding.

Acknowledgments

No book is ever written by just one or two people. We would like to thank all those who believed in this project, inspired us, and helped us to share the powerful impact of Birth Order Personality.

Agent extraordinaire Barbara Doyen saw the potential in this concept before anyone and brought us all together. Barbara, you are as wonderful as you are talented. We kiss your feet.

Special thanks also to Dr. Douglas Johnson, psychiatrist and Transactional Analysis trainer, for his great teaching ability; Dr. Taibi Kahler for his work with mini-scripts, which led to the Birth Order Personality discovery; the six thousand-plus clients who shared their hearts and lives with Cliff Isaacson and enabled him to formulate his Birth Order Personality concept; Dr. Michael McNeill, a good friend and terrific counselor; Lisa Reuter, graphic artist and true friend, who helped us with the illustrations and charts in this book, and Steve Williams, who helped with the T-shirt illustrations.

Lastly, we both owe our families more thanks than the world can hold for supporting us while we immersed ourselves in this consuming project.

So Kathy Isaacson, Duane, Mary, Shirley, Linda, Kevin, Andrew, and Rachel—this is your book, too. Your love and support continue to keep us centered.

Introduction

The psychology of Birth Order is an ever-evolving system of personal discovery. Ordinary people do extraordinary things using Birth Order. For example, a Third Born man improved his marriage by understanding Birth Order. He learned that he talked in terms of conclusions, but did not share the thoughts that led to these conclusions. He just stated the bottom line of his thinking.

He is married to a Second Born who loves details. Because of his form of communication, he was not sharing details with her. She was becoming discontent in the marriage. Wisely, they sought help and learned about Birth Order.

When the husband realized what he was doing to make his wife unhappy, he changed his ways. Because it was not natural for him to share details, he started making notations in a pocket notebook about things that happened during his day at work, things he heard, and thoughts he had. On the way home he reviewed his notes so that he was prepared to talk details to his wife when he got home.

She became happy, and the marriage was saved.

Sometimes the solutions to problems are simple when you know Birth Order. An Only Child woman, married to a Fourth Born husband, could not understand why he became angry when he walked in the door at the end of the day. She had the house cleaned, and everything was in order before he arrived. When he got home she was seated with a cup of coffee in front of the television. He never noticed that the house was clean, and was not aware of how hard she worked to get it that way.

Through Birth Order she came to know that he despised laziness. It looked to him like she was being lazy sitting in front of the television when he came home. So, she changed her tactics. Instead of sitting, she would be working when he came home. His reaction turned to appreciation. Ten minutes later she could sit down before the television and enjoy her coffee, and it was okay with him.

Another woman had a different problem. She was married to a Second Born man who reacted to the house being a mess when he got home. Their four children created chaos in the house, making it impossible for her to keep the house as neat as he wanted.

Through Birth Order she learned that he was a perfectionist. It was very hard for him to accept a messy house. He got irritable when he saw toys scattered about, clothes lying here and there, and disarray in the house.

So, she devised a strategy of cleaning the house just before he came home so that it was the way he wanted when he walked in the door. Their children were able to play freely during the day, creating the mess, which she cleaned up all at once just before he got home. Later in the evening the house became messy, but he felt good because he had seen it when it was neat.

Understanding Birth Order is like understanding algebra. Once you grasp it you can use it just like algebra to figure out things—in this case, human nature. Birth Order principles illustrate the facets of personality in ways that no personality test can. I would not trade my knowledge of Birth Order for the best training in psychological testing. Birth Order works better and is certainly much faster and more reliable.

The major setting in which I have used Birth Order is in

counseling. My clients have been the beneficiaries of Birth Order discoveries and have contributed to the discoveries with their own candid revelations. In counseling we are able to do useful interventions in the very first session, because it takes so little time to determine a person's Birth Order Personality. Interventions are effective because they are targeted to the personality of the person. Problems are clarified through the understanding of Birth Order, and relationships are enhanced.

The major benefit to relationships is the change from judging to feeling compassion. Once you understand Birth Order Personality, you can be understanding of the foibles of others without condemning them for being the way they are. You understand that people do not do things "on purpose" when they are acting out of Birth Order Personality. In our society we tend to think that everyone has a choice when they do what they do—except, sometimes, ourselves. Yet we can be very hard on both others and ourselves when we don't acknowledge that some behavior is actually the result of Birth Order Personality.

The attitude toward people who commit crimes may change when we realize that people do what they are programmed to do by their Birth Order. We might change our criminal system from punitive to redemptive. We might choose to incarcerate people to protect society, rather than as a corrective measure to change their behavior.

Birth Order knowledge can also be a boon in the marketplace. In one of my seminars a businessman learned that Third Born Personalities make the best salespeople. He put that knowledge into practice, hiring two new salespeople on this basis. He was amazed and said that the Third Borns were chomping at the bit to start seeing customers before he had even finished training them. His business ended up prospering from these super salespeople he put in the field.

I have also conducted a number of Birth Order

Personality seminars for nurses. Nurses are intermediaries between doctors and patients, carrying out the doctor's orders with the patients. This can be difficult emotionally for the nurse if the doctor is brusque or if the patient is recalcitrant, and often both are the case. Sometimes, the nurse can see a better way of dealing with a patient than what a doctor has ordered.

Life at work has become easier for nurses through Birth Order. When faced with a frightened Third Born Personality patient, for example, the nurse will know to respond to the fear with reassurance that he or she will be there for the Third Born. That is the easy one.

Nurses have also learned how to deal with the difficult patient who complains all the time; the patient who becomes more comfortable from knowing the details; the patient who never complains even when he or she should; and the patient who is overly emotional. Then, of course there are the visitors. The difficult ones reveal their Birth Order Personality by the way they act, giving the nurse an idea of how to interact with them. An understanding of Birth Order Personality equips nurses to deal with the various ways that people come at them in the hospital setting.

In the area of parenting, the knowledge of Birth Order Personality is also a great help. It would become apparent to parents, for example, that threats cannot change behavior that is Birth Order driven. Parents who recognize Birth Order traits will be much more patient with their children and will realize how futile it is to try to force each child into the same kind of mold. Those who recognize that personality differences are due to Birth Order will not make the mistake of comparing children to each other.

Not so long ago, the parents of an eleven-year-old boy came to me for help in dealing with their son. They wanted me to meet one-on-one with their son, but I convinced them to come see me first.

After talking with them, I discovered their son's Birth Order Personality, which I explained to them. I also determined their own Birth Order Personalities, and described to them how their Personalities could influence the way they interacted with their son, as well as the probable causes of problems with him. They asked if they should bring their son to the next session, but I asked them to wait because I wanted them to learn more about their own Personalities.

Next time the couple came we did more of the same, and they really enjoyed learning about Birth Order. People love to learn about themselves and this couple was surprised at the details I was able to surmise about them. Since I felt that there was still more to explain with the couple before I saw their son, I suggested they come in one more time. By the third time I saw them, however, they told me that their son no longer needed to see me because he was doing so well! The parents had been able to bring needed changes themselves by understanding how Birth Order Personality rules our lives.

Birth Order knowledge can help to make parenting so much easier and more effective by helping parents to understand their children and their own relationships with them. I find that one of the most gratifying aspects of using Birth Order to counsel is the knowledge that the effects will continue through to the next generation. I like to think that children who have never seen me will end up benefiting from these counseling sessions.

Children of all ages are actually able to learn about Birth Order Personality. One Fourth Born, an admittedly precocious four-year-old, said to her brother, "You are such a First Born," when he was behaving like a First Born by teasing her. This actually got him to think about what he had been doing, and he stopped his teasing. This girl had a grasp of what Birth Order is all about by learning about it from her mother. Imagine how well she will interact with people as a grownup, with the knowledge of Birth Order being second nature to her!

As the four-year-old may have guessed, understanding Birth Order can help you to create empathy in others. For example, in one workplace the supervisor's Birth Order caused her to be oblivious to the way others felt. One day, after the supervisor had inadvertently hurt another employee's feelings, one employee who knew about Birth Order had a word with her. He was able to explain to the supervisor just how badly the employee felt, in such a way that the supervisor was moved from being a cold, logical, critical person to a compassionate and caring person. This is an excellent example of how "magic words" can be used with each Birth Order Personality to bring about mutual understanding, improve communication, and create effective confrontation when necessary.

What is the future of Birth Order? It boggles the mind. Since Birth Order defines relationships, it has the potential to change the ways in which people interact—from diplomacy between nations to casual conversation on the street. It can also offer new ways of teaching and learning so as to maximize education, and it can help locate the psychological roots of emotional and physical illness for greater health. Birth Order can also increase the effectiveness of mass communication by enabling the communicator to speak to each person in the psychological language he or she needs to hear.

When Birth Order Personality becomes widely understood the manipulators among us will lose their power. In the past, these types of people have been able to prey upon our ignorance of ourselves and our weaknesses. Once we truly understand ourselves we can transcend the weaknesses of our personalities, which will allow us to sidestep those that would try to victimize us. Truly, there is power in knowing.

Does everyone want to know about Birth Order? Some

would reject it out of hand because they "don't want to be put in a box." Although this may seem to have some merit, the fact is that we already live in a box. Rather than putting you in a box, Birth Order knowledge gives you the tools to find your way out of the box.

When I graduated from high school so many years ago, I gave the valedictory speech. It was not long—only about three minutes—but preparing for it took quite some time. I put much thought and lots of agonizing into it. This was to be a glorious moment I wanted to cherish so it had to be just right. In that speech I expressed one thought that has stayed with me all my life: I told the audience that when I came to the end of my life I wanted to be able to look back and say that I had helped make the world a better place.

Sharing this knowledge of Birth Order fulfills that desire. I am so happy to be able to pass it on to you; may it make your world a better place to be.

—Cliff Isaacson

When I discover who I am,
I'll be free.
—Ralph Ellison

Chapter One

The Birth of Birth Order

It was evident from his slumped shoulders and shuffling gait that the man coming through the front door was upset. He only lifted his head slightly when Cliff Isaacson ushered him through the foyer and into his office, closing the door quietly behind them. For Isaacson, closing the door was a gesture that was meant to imply a promise of confidentiality, of caring, of listening, and, usually, of change and growth.

As a minister and therapist, Isaacson spent his days and nights caring for his own congregation, as well as for other men, women, and children throughout the community who knew of his work as a counselor. That evening, when he asked his visitor to sit down, Isaacson had no idea that he was about to change the man's life and his own in a way that would eventually affect thousands of others.

Moments after Isaacson sat down himself, the man began sobbing. Isaacson quickly discovered that the married thirty-four-year-old father of two had left his wife in a fit of rage.

"I was so angry," the man told Isaacson, with tears rolling down his face. "I shouted at her and then I left and the last thing I said was, 'File for divorce. This marriage is over.'"

Isaacson looked at the man and his own mind went into overdrive. He needed to know more, but he was already certain that he could help the man in front of him.

"Tell me everything," Isaacson told his client. "Why were you angry?"

The story was a simple one. His wife had gone out shopping and had stopped afterwards to have a cup of coffee with a girlfriend she had bumped into at the grocery store. When she was late getting home the man had assumed that she'd seen another man. In fact, he told Isaacson that he was constantly worried that someone more handsome, smarter, or richer would take his wife away from him.

"I'm angry," admitted the man. "If she is gone longer than a few minutes or goes out with friends or anything like that, I just assume I'm losing her and that someone else will fall in love with her."

Isaacson wanted his client to keep talking, and the man, obviously in great emotional pain, was eager to talk. He said he loved his wife very much and knew that she loved him, but he was constantly overcome with feelings that he didn't understand.

As his client told Isaacson his life story, something began clicking into place in Isaacson's mind. The man said that he was the youngest of seven brothers and that, when he was a child, his brothers had always been able to take away his toys whenever they wanted. As he grew older they did the same thing with his girlfriends. When Isaacson made a connection between the man's birth order and his constant feelings of anger and fear, he smiled and his thoughts became clear. He knew exactly what to do.

Isaacson, who had been slowly discovering unique birth order patterns in his patients as well as in his own five children, saw that evening that his ideas about a birth order that was psychological in its origins—not chronologicial—could change lives and help others.

Isaacson explained to the client that he probably still felt as if he lived in a world of older brothers who could take things from him any time they wanted. "You are an adult among adults now," he told the man. "You are no longer a boy among older brothers who can take away your wife."

He also made it clear to the man that his wife had chosen him, that she had a mind of her own, and that no one could take her away unless she wanted it to happen. "Your big brothers are gone now," Isaacson said.

Once the client realized that his feelings of jealousy had taken root in his early family life and were unnecessary in his present circumstances, he was able to let go of them. The man went back to his wife that night and they talked for hours. He came back to see Isaacson a week later to say that his life had drastically changed and that he was no longer afraid to let his wife out of his sight. Six months later, Isaacson received a Christmas card from the man thanking him. "I have a new life," he wrote.

The night when Isaacson got his distraught client to talk about birth order, he was tapping into his own subconscious resources. Those resources had been building and moving Isaacson closer to his new Birth Order theory for years.

Since that time, Isaacson has worked with thousands of people and has effectively treated them with that theory. With each client, Isaacson was able to refine his Birth Order profiles, and time and time again his insights into Birth Order Personality proved to be correct and therapeutically helpful. As a result, his counseling services have changed lives, opened hearts, and, most important, opened up a new world of understanding to those who learn about it.

In this day of mass marketing and public relations, Isaacson and his associates manage to fill their available counseling hours simply by word of mouth. His success is based in the fact that he's offering the world something positive, something new, and something that can lift the lid on behavior, attitudes, and the feelings of confusion that often make it difficult for people to enjoy the good stuff in life.

Imagine a world where people are able to look at themselves and others with a new level of understanding and acceptance. That is exactly what Birth Order Personality allows us all to do. It is a simple, easy-to-understand concept that can be put to use on a daily basis by anyone interested in better knowing themselves and the people who live in their world.

Imagine engaging in a simple conversation and within minutes being able to understand why a person thinks, acts, talks, loves, and feels the way they do. Imagine finally being able to see why your sister loves to skydive and why she was the only one in the family to have the guts to go into the Tower of Terror in Disney World. (The answer would be that she's a Third Born.) Imagine understanding why your first marriage broke up, why it was impossible for you to blend your life with someone who was a psychological "Only Child." Imagine being able to motivate the son who drives you crazy every morning with his rebelliousness by saying something as simple as the word "please."

> "I used to think anyone doing anything weird was weird. Now I know that it is the people that call others weird that are weird."
>
> —Paul McCartney

Once Isaacson realized that there was indeed a psychological Birth Order that motivated, compelled, and guided every single person in the world, he knew that he could use that knowledge to help himself and to help others.

So what is this new form of Birth Order? you may be

asking. Where did it come from and why is it a concept that can add something positive to even the most well adjusted person's life?

The Origins of the Birth Order Theory

Cliff Isaacson's journey toward understanding the Birth Order Personality, like many discoveries, did not happen overnight, even though his first Birth Order counseling session had seen close to immediate success. Isaacson had unknowingly begun gathering the pieces of his Birth Order puzzle for years, as he studied the habits and patterns of the people he dealt with as a Methodist minister. His role as the leader of his church had naturally led him to offer counseling and guidance services.

In 1969, when he took a position as an associate pastor of a large Methodist Church in Iowa, Isaacson was introduced to Transactional Analysis via a psychiatrist who was offering a clinic at a local mental health center. This form of analysis became popular in the 1960s when psychiatrist Eric Berne defined human nature in three parts: the parent, the child, and the adult. A portion of Transactional Analysis includes five mini-scripts, or patterns, by which people live their lives, known as "Hurry up," "Please Me," "Be Perfect," "Be Strong," and "Try Hard." Isaacson soon began using those scripts when dealing with his own five children—each child, in fact, seemed to fit one of the scripts perfectly.

Isaacson's oldest son, Duane, was a major hit in school, always impressing the teachers. From day one Duane was goal-oriented and would never back down when the going got tough. Duane, as his father would discover, was and remains a classic First Born Birth Order Personality. A jazz musician, Duane also works with horses and is known for his ability to train horses that others may have abandoned.

Mary, the second oldest, who was a perfectionist from the day she started walking, was and remains a serious Second Born Birth Order Personality. When Mary was a little girl, she made her mother tie her shoelaces so that the bows were exactly even. If her mother failed to make perfect little bows, Mary would insist they be done over. Now married and an excellent parent (a Second Born trait), Mary has a reputation for being a dependable and competent administrator. When she moved back to Iowa from Florida to be closer to her parents, Isaacson wasn't surprised, because the need for Mary to be close to her parents is a deep-seated Second Born trait.

Isaacson's Third Born Birth Order Personality is his fearless daughter Shirley. Third Borns, like Shirley, will try anything. When she was a little girl, Shirley followed her big brother, climbing to the top of a tree while her sisters watched. Shirley also has a compassionate Third Born streak that led her to give away clothes in high school and to befriending all of her ignored classmates. Once she lent a beautiful new jacket that had never been worn to a girl who wanted to wear it to the homecoming parade.

The Fourth Born Personality Isaacson child, Linda, has loved challenges from toddlerhood. This Fourth Born trait is a constant that shows up as Fourth Borns take on positions and tackle jobs that others may stay away from. When she was four years old, Linda taught herself to read by playing with a typewriter. Today she uses her highly developed computer skills to create textbooks for a book publisher.

Although Kevin was chronologically born fifth in the Isaacson family, he is actually an Only Child psychologically. Kevin is a magnificent organizer, and when he was in second grade he managed to put together a major football game between two schools in different towns. (The home team lost because Kevin's dad, who was the coach, had a hard time holding the ball himself, but everyone had a good time.) One of Kevin's other Only Child characteristics manifested during childhood was his love of being alone. He deeply enjoyed being in his room by himself, whether it was to do his homework, practice his guitar, or watch sports on television.

As Isaacson began counseling as part of his TA training, he would ask his clients about their birth order and noticed that amazing patterns began to develop. By comparing his clients to his own five children, Isaacson could tell he was on to something. Soon he was picking up common sayings and behaviors of Only Children, First Borns, Second Borns, Third Borns, and Fourth Borns. He also discovered that those Birth Order patterns could repeat themselves within a family.

It became obvious to Isaacson that there were just five Birth Orders: Only Child, First Born, Second Born, Third Born, and Fourth Born. It also became clear to him that there are exceptions to the general rule that Birth Order Personality usually corresponds to one's chronological birth order. For example, a chronological second born could actually have a Third Born Personality, and a sixth child could psychologically be an Only Child. Birth Order Personality is influenced by both the birth order of a sibling and the environment into which the child is born.

Isaacson discovered early on that there could be a great difference between a client's chronological birth order and psychological Birth Order. He was more than familiar with the chronological birth order ideas that had been popularized by psychiatrist Alfred Adler, who had developed the idea of a first, middle, and youngest child. This birth order program put everyone inside of a tidy box according to chronology and insisted that the parents and the gender of the child offered the greatest influence in determining a child's birth order.

That box was a confining spot. For example, those labeled as oldest children in the Adlerian birth order would be expected to be perfectionists because it was believed that they were constantly trying to act and think like their parents. It's pretty tough to ever grow up to be an adult yourself if you are carrying all that first-born weight on your shoulders.

Isaccson not only perceived that the old birth order ideas were confining, he also saw clearly that they didn't work. He could identify dozens of men and women who simply didn't fit into this birth order plan. Isaacson's own Birth Order discoveries agreed with Adler's theories in only one area: Birth order really does influence personality. Switch on a light in a dark room and your view of nothing becomes a view of everything—which is what it is like to compare the old way of thinking about birth order and the new way of thinking.

Have you ever met someone at a dinner party, in a waiting room, at a soccer game, or in the local bar and within minutes of meeting that person, the two of you are talking as if you were old friends? Have you ever come home and said, "Honey, I just met someone who thinks the same way that I think?" Do you have a friend who likes to go to the same places you do, who looks at other people the same way—maybe even walks the same way you do? Most likely, this person has the same psychological Birth Order as you. Maybe your college roommate was a detailed Second Born who agreed with you that all the empty beer bottles in your dorm room should be lined up on the shelves. Or maybe you met a friend through church who possesses the same Only Child sarcastic sense of humor. Perhaps you work with another First Born who agrees with your own First Born tendencies to do loads of research when writing a report or acquiring a new client.

Once Isaacson discovered Birth Order Personality, specific behaviors of his family and friends suddenly made sense, and he began to be able to quickly identify behavior problems of his clients. Consider Darlene, for example.

Darlene was a 62-year-old retired schoolteacher who

couldn't quite connect the dots of her own life but was worried about everyone else south of Canada. She also had a very loud voice.

"Cliff," she bellowed into the phone. "It's Darlene."

Isaacson smiled on the other end of the line and thought to himself that it was a waste of time for Darlene to have to identify herself. "Hi, Darlene," he said, "how are you?"

"Forget about me," she barked, "have you helped Henry yet? Were you able to help him get a job?"

Oh, man, thought Isaacson, here she goes worrying about the world when she's got more than her own share of problems!

"Darlene," he said calmly, in his smooth therapist voice, "first of all, I have no idea how to help a scientist find a job, and secondly, Henry hasn't asked me to help him find a job."

"What?" Darlene asked, astonishment in her voice. "What?" she asked again just to make certain Cliff was listening.

"He didn't ask for help," Isaacson said again.

Now Darlene was a bit angry. "You mean to tell me you don't help people unless they ask?"

"That's right," Isaacson said, and then he paused for just a second, took a deep breath, and added, "For example, you need help and you haven't asked."

This had the effect of striking Darlene dumb. Cliff Isaacson had said just the right thing to get the attention of a Fourth Born like Darlene. His Birth Order strategies had shown him that Fourth Borns like to come on strong, all the time hoping that you will react to them in the same way and make a connection. Isaacson knew that if he had backed off when the strong-willed Darlene began barking at him, he would've gotten absolutely nowhere with her.

His approach had sure worked with Darlene. He couldn't even hear her breathing on the other end of the phone line.

"Darlene, do you want to come in to see me?"

"Yes," she answered in a whisper. "Yes, I want to come in and see you."

Not only did Darlene come in to see Isaacson, but she brought along a book of poetry that she would pick up and read to him every time she felt a twinge of stress. But once Fourth Born Darlene got the hang of helping herself and opening up, she was unstoppable. She attended group therapy, went on to see a psychiatrist, and ended up with a smile on her face and a life that she finally thought was worth living. She did, however, continue to yell into the phone—but it was with gusto and joy, not because she was constantly trying to get someone's attention.

Isaacson had found that the attributes of each Birth Order were so clear and concise, it was nothing short of astonishing. Parenting, friendship, and marriage styles were also identical in each Birth Order category. Soon Isaacson was able to determine a person's psychological Birth Order by noting something as simple as his or her sense of humor.

Isaacson also saw, however, that the similarities apparent in people with the same Birth Order Personality went far beyond the telling of a joke. In fact, the many common denominators he found enabled him to formulate charts and questions designed to help his clients understand why they acted and reacted the way they did.

Once Isaacson convinced himself that Birth Order meant far more than a child's position in a family, he began to define psychological Birth Order profiles by drawing upon the personalities identified by Transactional Analysis. Essentially, he eliminated the theory about the "middle child," established that the First Born child could be found anywhere within a family's makeup, and gave the youngest child a Birth Order Personality. Central to his concept of psychological Birth Order was the idea that one's date and time of birth were far less important than one's thought patterns, ways of speaking, and personality—the individual, glorious, wonderful personality.

By the mid-1980s Isaacson was counseling as much as possible and trying hard to maintain his full-time work as a minister. He loved counseling so much that he gave up fishing and gardening and his precious ham radio. His new addiction—counseling with his Birth Order strategies—was more rewarding than anything he had ever done in his life.

In 1986, with the help of some good friends, Isaacson started the Upper Des Moines Counseling Center. Since he had started counseling, and especially since he began developing his Birth Order strategies, he had become a man with a mission. Helping people and spreading the gospel of Birth Order became his number one passion and the counseling center was a way for him to follow his heart.

> "Be who you are and say what you feel, because those who mind don't matter and those who matter don't mind."
>
> —Dr. Seuss

By turning his hobby into his vocation, Isaacson was able to devote all his time to writing, lecturing, and teaching seminars based on his new Birth Order theory. He was also touching lives in a way that astounded other counselors and therapists—who, in turn, began using the Birth Order techniques themselves.

Isaacson viewed his clients as a resource for his Birth Order research. As he first began developing an understanding of the five personality traits, he had to constantly use his own children as reference points. By forming a picture of one of his children in his mind, and of how he or she thought and acted, he was able to see the Birth Order similarities in others. Gradually, however, as he became more and more familiar with personalities and Birth Order, he was able to abandon the practice of using his children as Birth Order models and could tell remarkably fast which Birth Order a person fit into.

From the beginning, Isaacson did not focus on Birth

Order as a method or means of change; he was simply using it as a tool for understanding. Once he was able to determine a person's Birth Order Personality through a series of questions, by observing his or her behavior, and by simply getting the person to talk and share what was in his or her heart, he would design a way for that client to look at his or her own traits in a nonthreatening manner. As a result, his clients were able to look at themselves nonjudgmentally in terms of Birth Order rather than in terms of having a specific personality problem. Isaacson realized that it would be more helpful for someone to hear, "John, did you know that Fourth Borns are really stubborn and have a difficult time letting go of something?" rather than, "John, you are really stubborn and you never give in."

Instead of feeling as if they had been personally attacked, clients could see that Isaacson was merely taking an objective look at their personality. Birth Order became a very nonthreatening way of giving people feedback. The above-mentioned John, for example, could look at himself and think, "Geeze, there must be lots of Fourth Borns out there who act like this. We can't be all that bad, but maybe, I can still be a Fourth Born and not be so darned angry."

Isaacson uses Birth Order to give others a sense of their own potential. Once people see themselves as a specific Birth Order Personality, they can be and become whatever they want. They can throw away the bad and the ugly and keep the good stuff, then get on with building a life that holds more than they ever thought possible.

It became obvious to Isaacson early on that if everyone understood the concepts of Birth Order, life would be a bit easier for all of us. Imagine a mother trying desperately to understand why her daughter likes to jump off the swing set, always brings home the kids in class who have no friends, and is constantly challenging her orders. If that mother knew she was dealing with a classic, risk-taking, kindhearted Third

Born daughter who had a creative streak a mile wide and was not intentionally disobeying her mother, wouldn't her life be easier? Oh, yeah, you know it would be easier.

How about the wife trying to understand why in the world her Only Child husband loves to be alone in the garage and runs for a pencil every time some expert on television gives advice on anything from gutters or tire rotation to relationships. Hey, this guy isn't trying to drive his bride crazy, he's just being an Only Child who loves to spend time alone and to follow the advice of experts.

Then there is the employee with a Fourth Born boss who refuses to help him with a report because he thinks the employee is lazy, and is so controlling that he wants to know when the employee goes to the bathroom. This Fourth Born will drive the entire office crazy unless everyone understands his need for control, his view of life as being hard, and his ability underneath all of that to empathize with you anyway.

Understanding Birth Order is like having a magic key that unlocks any door you want to pass through. Parents will be able to better understand their children, and children who believe that their parents understand them will have a view of life that is incredibly positive. Employers can use Birth Order knowledge to help them assign jobs and responsibility. By knowing an employee's strengths and assigning positions accordingly, the employer and the employee will both be more productive.

Birth Order Personality understanding can help you purchase a car, work with a repairperson, talk to your child's math teacher, and handle that irritating relative who has managed to drive you up a wall for the past twenty-five years. Understanding how and why people think and feel the way they do is not only a valuable tool, it's a gift.

This book is offering you a new way of thinking; what you do with it is up to you. It is important to remember that there are no good or bad Birth Orders, and that, no matter which Birth Order you claim, no two Second Borns or Third Borns or any borns are exactly alike. The way you raise your eyebrows, your own particular smile, and the way you can charm the socks off of anyone you care to—hey, that's what makes you you.

All you have to do now is to unwrap this huge present. Take the ribbon off, pull back the wrapping, and first have a look at yourself. Learn about your own Birth Order Personality, understand it, and then turn this knowledge into a form of understanding that will walk you right into a happier life. Turn the page and see if you can find yourself in the Only Child, First Born, Second Born, Third Born, or Fourth Born descriptions and definitions that follow.

Knowing is half the battle.
—GI Joe

Chapter Two

I'm a What?

Are you ready for some serious work? What about some even more serious answers? This is the place to set aside all you have ever heard, or thought, about chronological birth order. Wrap it all up and put it away in some drawer, because you are about to embark on an adventure that will forever change how you look at and feel about yourself and everyone else in your life.

Many of us grew up with misplaced ideas about who we are and why we behave the way we do. Parents may have said, "You are the first-born, so you will be in charge. You know you are the responsible one." A second child could have been raised to think that she was helpless because of her chronological birth order. An only child might spend years thinking he is selfish and ill-behaved because "that's how only children behave." While those views are true in the sense that a first-born will always be a chronological first-born, they do not hold true when it comes to Birth Order Personality.

There is a commonality among people who share the same Birth Order Personality. A woman with a First Born Birth Order Personality will be linked via her personality characteristics to other First Born Personalities throughout the universe. That's how simple it is. Those with a certain Birth Order Personality may exhibit variety in certain ways they express themselves, but the Personality characteristics—the thinking patterns, emotional dynamics, and style of interaction with others—is always the same beneath each individual smile, walk, or laugh. That's why it is so easy to gain a better understanding of the people you interact with on a daily basis, once you've learned about Birth Order Personality.

Think about it this way: hold out your hand in front of your face and think about the fact that you have four fingers and a thumb. The fingerprints vary, but a thumb is always a thumb. There is no way that baby is ever going to become an index finger. It's always going to be sticking out like a thumb and acting like a thumb. The same is true for Birth Order Personalities. Once an Only Child always an Only Child—which is pretty darn comforting if you think about it.

It also makes sense that the Birth Order Personalities of our parents affect us. If a chronological third-born son spends countless hours with a stay-at-home third-born mother, it makes sense that the son would inherit some of the mother's Third Born Personality traits. Chapter 10 deals with secondary characteristics that play a role in Birth Order Personality. This may sound complicated now, but Chapter 10 will give you concrete charts to keep these characteristics in focus.

For now, we are going to concentrate on figuring out who you really are. These simple and fun Birth Order Personality tests can show you how to answer that question and other questions you may have about yourself.

There are a few prerequisites that must be followed before you pick up a pen and get to work. First of all, remember that everything in this book—every page, every word, every test—has been written to further your understanding. There are no right or wrong answers, and there are no right or wrong—or good or bad—Birth Order Personalities. Just keep an open mind as you think about the answers, and answer each question honestly.

Many people struggle with new concepts. Don't be surprised if it takes you time to process what you are learning, simply because this is something new and something that does not fit in with other chronological birth order concepts. Go slowly, and think about what you are reading. Try and imagine yourself in a whole new light. Focus on your good characteristics first. Are you kind? Do you love to help people? Always keep in mind that this should be a positive experience. There isn't anyone waiting in the wings to point out something terrible about you and your personality. By looking at yourself as a specific Birth Order Personality, you will slowly begin to see how you were formed and why you do things the way that you do them.

It may also help you to think about someone close to you as you begin processing this information. As the Birth Order Personalities come into focus, it will become clear to you that your husband is an Only Child, for example, or that your mother was a true Second Born. Once you can put a face on a specific Birth Order Personality, the entire concept will become much clearer to you. It makes sense that once you grasp your own Personality, the Personality of someone you live with, love, or are close to at work will also become clear to you. That is a good way to begin to understand this new way of thinking.

Take your time. Some of the questions may seem simple, but be certain you put some mental energy into thinking about how you act and react. Remember those grade-school teachers who told you that your first response to an answer is usually the correct response? That holds true for this series of tests as well. Go with your gut—which is actually not that far from your heart.

It will also help if you gather the input of a few people who are close to you—a spouse, parent, sibling, friends—while you work on finding the answers to the following questions. Others often tend to see many of our personality character-istics clearer than we do ourselves. If you don't have help with the tests there is a good chance they may not be accu-rate, in which case you will be disillusioned and will have to start all over again.

Have fun. Although *The Birth Order Effect* offers some serious and potentially life-changing answers for those who choose to accept this look at themselves, it should be a journey that is as much fun as it is challenging.

Go find your favorite spot in the house. Turn on some music. Get your favorite beverage. Clear your mind and get to work. You are going to have a ball—honest.

Birth Order Personality Inventory

Identifying Your Psychological Birth Order

There are five Personalities according to Birth Order. Your personality may or may not correspond to your actual place in the family. The following inventory allows you to determine your psychological Birth Order Personality.

Instructions: Choose the answer that most closely fits one of the four options given. When finished, enter your scores on the form at the end of the inventory. Do the calculations to identify your psychological Birth Order.

The accuracy of the test is enhanced if you answer the questions as you would have answered them in your late teens or early twenties. (Behaviors learned as you mature can obscure Birth Order characteristics that were apparent when you were younger.)

1 = never; 2 = sometimes; 3 = often; 4 = always

1. Do you have to organize before you can do something?　　1 ②3 4

2. Do you want to impress others?　　1 2 ③ 4

3. Do you try to avoid feeling inadequate?　　1 2 3 ④

4. Did you feel life was unfair as a child?　　1 2 3 ④

5. Do you like difficult challenges?　　1 ②3 4

6. Do you make "to do" lists?　　① 2 3 4

7. Do you say, "I don't know"?　　1 ②3 4

8. Do you pay attention to details?　　1 2 3 ④

9. Do you avoid doing things that scare you?　　1 2 ③ 4

10. Do you distrust people?　　1 2 ③ 4

11. Do you operate from a schedule in your mind?　　① 2 3 4

12. Are you careful not to offend others?　　1 2 3 ④

13. Do you suppress feelings?　　1 2 3 ④

14. Do you try to act like nothing bothers you?　　1 2 3 ④

15. Do you try to prove how mature you are?　　① 2 3 4

16. Do you think with your feelings?　　1 2 ③ 4

17. Do you rehearse what you will say?　　1 ② 3 4

18. Do you look for what is wrong with things?　　1 2 ③ 4

19. Is it important for you to be strong?　　1 ② 3 4

20. Do you feel like you are not wanted?　　1 2 3 ④

21. Do you feel bad when others feel bad?　　1 2 ③ 4

22. Do you feel guilty?　　1 ② 3 4

23. Do you say, "I would appreciate it if you would . . . "?　　1 ② 3 4

24. Do you relate well to victims?　　1 2 3 ④

25. Do you resent being asked for favors?　　1 2 ③ 4

26. Do you interrupt when others are talking?　　1 ② 3 4

27. Do you rehash past encounters?　　1 2 ③ 4

1 = never; 2 = sometimes; 3 = often; 4 = always

28. Do you say, "That's not necessary"? (okay)   ① 2 3 ④

29. Do you jump to conclusions?   1 2 3 ④

30. Do you try to avoid being trapped?   1 2 ③ 4

31. Do you worry about family and friends?   1 2 ③ 4

32. Do you think people should get what they deserve? 1 ② 3 4

33. Do you like giving constructive criticism?   1 ② 3 4

34. Do you compare things?   1 2 ③ 4

35. Do you feel left out?   1 2 ③ 4

36. Do you wish for time at home alone?   1 2 ③ 4

37. Do you try to impress other people rather than   1 ② 3 4
     just doing your own thing?

38. Do you focus on details when there is no need   1 2 3 ④
     to do so?

39. Are you afraid people can put you down   1 2 3 ④
     whenever they want?

40. Do you hate being blamed?   1 2 3 ④

41. Do you dislike being interrupted?   1 2 3 ④

42. Are you nice to people rather than honest?   1 2 3 ④

43. Do you dislike deadlines?   1 2 3 ④

44. Do you say, "No problem!"?   1 2 ③ 4

45. Do you feel no one understands you?   1 2 3 ④

46. Do you feel you can't do what you want?   1 2 ③ 4

47. Do you have trouble expressing love?   1 2 3 ④

48. Are you overwhelmed by emotion?   1 ② 3 4

49. Do you like to help others?   1 ② 3 4

50. Do you analyze things from all sides?   ① 2 3 4

51. Are you afraid of appearing spoiled?   ① 2 3 4

52. Is it difficult for you to accept love?   1 ② 3 4

53. Do you prefer projects to goals?   1 2 3 ④

1 = never; 2 = sometimes; 3 = often; 4 = always

54. Do you feel hurt when your idea is rejected?   1 2 3 (4)

55. Do you try to avoid answering questions for   1 2 (3) 4
    fear of being trapped?

56. Do you feel weighted down?   1 2 (3) 4

57. Do you fear people will be hard on you?   1 2 3 (4)

58. Do you give praise indirectly?   (1) 2 (3) 4

59. Do you keep busy to keep from being bored?   (1) 2 3 4

60. Do you feel like no one listens?   1 2 (3) 4

61. Do you do small projects first?   1 (2) 3 4

62. Do you feel compelled to agree?   1 2 3 (4)

63. Do you feel like nothing is good enough?   1 2 3 (4)

64. Do you get angry when told to do things?   1 (2) 3 4

65. Do you try to control your anger?   1 2 3 (4)

66. Do you get upset when people drop in without   1 2 (3) 4
    letting you know they are coming?

67. Do you hint for what you want?   1 2 (3) 4

68. Does it make you angry when someone   1 2 3 (4)
    accuses you of being nasty?

69. Do you share your ideas with other people   1 (2) (3) 4
    because you want to please them?

70. Do you hate laziness?   1 (2) 3 4

71. Does life feel like all work and no play?   1 (2) 3 4

72. Do you compromise?   1 2 (3) 4

73. Are you a peacemaker?   1 2 3 (4)

74. Do you hate being cornered?   1 2 3 (4)

75. Do you get angry when others do nothing?   (1)(2) 3 4

Coding Instructions

Enter the number you selected for each inventory question below.

	A		B		C		D		E
1:	2	2:	3	3:	4	4:	4	5:	2
6:	1	7:	2	8:	4	9:	3	10:	3
11:	1	12:	4	13:	4	14:	4	15:	1
16:	3	17:	2	18:	3	19:	2	20:	3
21:	3	22:	2	23:	2	24:	4	25:	3
26:	2	27:	3	28:	4	29:	4	30:	3
31:	3	32:	2	33:	2	34:	3	35:	3
36:	3	37:	2	38:	4	39:	4	40:	4
41:	4	42:	4	43:	4	44:	3	45:	4
46:	3	47:	3	48:	2	49:	2	50:	1
51:	1	52:	2	53:	4	54:	4	55:	3
56:	3	57:	4	58:	3	59:	1	60:	3
61:	2	62:	4	63:	4	64:	2	65:	4
66:	3	67:	3	68:	4	69:	3	70:	2
71:	2	72:	3	73:	4	74:	4	75:	2
Totals:	34		43		52		47		41

Your highest score indicates your psychological Birth Order:

A: ~~48~~ 34 = Only Child
B: ~~49~~ 43 = First Born
C: ~~48~~ 52 = Second Born
D: ~~49~~ 47 = Third Born
E: 41 41 = Fourth Born

Your next highest two scores indicate secondary Birth Order characteristics.

Wasn't that fun? How did you do? You are in there someplace and by now you should know where.

Here's another simple test that will help you determine your Birth Order Personality. This additional test will help you find your fit. Remember to be honest. Sometimes it may seem as if there is more than one correct answer. Take your time; the correct answer will make you say something like, "That's it!" Trust your feelings in selecting the answer that most closely applies to you.

Birth Order Assessment

---

1. If the following statements were printed on T-shirts, which would fit you the best?
   a. Front: I don't know; back: What do you think?
   b. Front: Life isn't easy; back: You have to try hard.
   c. Front: Leave me alone; back: I'd rather do it myself.
   d. Front: No problem; back: It doesn't bother me any.
   e. Front: That won't work; back: It's not good enough.

2. When you think, are you:
   a. Organizing?
   b. Evaluating?
   c. Analyzing?
   d. Comparing?
   e. Researching?

3. Which is your usual attitude?
   a. Life is not fair, so let's help the victims.
   b. Everyone should be given equal treatment.
   c. Don't get angry, get even.
   d. People should get what they deserve.
   e. The end justifies the means.

4. Which is your bad feeling?
   a. Loneliness
   b. Anxiety
   c. Guilt
   d. Inadequacy
   e. Pressure

5. What would bother you most in yourself?
   a. Shoddy workmanship
   b. Laziness
   c. A judgmental attitude
   d. Disorganization
   e. Insensitivity

6. In working, do you:
   a. Emphasize creativity?
   b. Pay attention to details?
   c. Make "to do" lists?
   d. Try hard?
   e. Feel relief whenever a job is done?

7. Which makes you the most ashamed?
   a. Appearing to have made a mistake
   b. Appearing to be guilty
   c. Appearing to be spoiled
   d. Appearing to be not grown up
   e. Appearing to be afraid

Scoring

Circle your answers for each question in the chart below. The column with the most answers circled represents your Birth Order Personality. If you feel it is incorrect, go over your answers with a friend to be sure they reflect your true Personality.

Question	Only Child	First	Second	Third	Fourth
1.	c	a	e	d	b
2.	a	e	b	d	c
3.	b	d	e	a	c
4.	e	c	d	b	a
5.	d	c	a	e	b
6.	c	e	b	a	d
7.	c	b	a	e	d

● ● ● ● ●

Three Rules of Work by Albert Einstein
1. Out of clutter, find simplicity.
2. From discord, find harmony.
3. In the middle of difficulty lies opportunity.

Chapter Three

The Birth Order Matrix

Still confused? Well, join the club. Understanding Birth Order Personality is not unlike learning algebra, how to hit the right tennis stroke, or how to be a good father. Sometimes it comes slowly. It takes lots of practice (and more than a little failure).

It may help to think about Birth Order Personality as something that is evolving every minute, every day of your life. As you come to know more about yourself and why you think and act the way you do, you will also get a clearer picture of Birth Order Personality. Those new insights will help you understand all of the Personalities, and that understanding will give you a new look at the world around you.

One of the greatest results of this new way of thinking is that it can be totally positive. *There are no good or bad Personalities.* Eventually, as you come to understand your own Birth Order Personality, it will be as if you have seen the reflection of your entire being. It's a wonderful, calming, magnificent experience.

Birth Order Personality, then, is the hand of cards that we have been dealt in our lives. We cannot change the cards in our hands—we can only choose how and when we will play them. Without knowledge of Birth Order Personality, people are playing their Birth Order cards with no rhyme or reason, and in the game of life that is not a good thing. It's like playing with your cards face down.

Coming to an understanding of Birth Order Personality is a lot like learning how to play the game of life the right way. As you make your way through *The Birth Order Effect* and begin turning your cards over, you will see that the game is even more exciting than you could have imagined. It's up to you to take the challenge.

The Birth Order Matrix is a terrific way to get started. It's something that you will probably use more than anything in this book and something that you can easily share with others who are up to the challenge of understanding Birth Order Personality.

The following set of pages has been designed to help you put various aspects of your personality into perspective. As with the preceding tests, it helps to take your time when you study the Birth Order matrixes.

You may find yourself laughing out loud as you stumble across something that really rings true about yourself or someone you know. If you find yourself slapping your head and saying, "That's me!" or "That's her!" it's a good sign. It means you are thinking, having a good time, and learning more about who you are.

These pages are also good reference points if you veer off course while you are reading the rest of the book. They are also lots of fun to take to parties. People will think you are a genius.

Birth Order Matrix

	Only Child	First Born	Second Born	Third Born	Fourth Born
Original Challenges	How to play alone without feeling lonely; intrusion	Loss of love to new baby; how to win the love back	Being outdone by the First Born; how to do well enough to be loved	Being picked on by Second Born; how to protect self	Being excluded by the Third Born
"Favorite" Bad Feeling	Frustration	Guilt	Inadequacy	Vulnerability	Anger
Coping Strategies	Imaginary friends; two speeds	Is placating; covers up	Perfectionism; logic	Is strong; uses aggression	Won't listen to self; tries hard
Felt Loss	Freedom	Love	Emotions	Defense	Belonging
Sense of Justice	Equality	Deserving	Necessity	Rescuing	Retaliation
Thought Patterns	Organization	Research	Evaluation	Comparison	Analysis
T-shirts	"Leave me alone; I'd rather do it myself!"	"I don't know; what do you think?"	"That won't work; it's not good enough."	"No problem; it doesn't bother me any."	"Life isn't easy; you have to try hard."

Birth Order Matrix: Relationships

	Only Child	First Born	Second Born	Third Born	Fourth Born
With Parents	Obedient, emotional	Demanding, competing	Close, deceiving	Helpful, rebellious	Uninvolved, secretive
Emotional Expression	Demonstrative	Flat, passive	Critical, intense	Sympathy, aggression	Empathy, withdrawal
Source of Anger	Intrusion	Lack of respect	Criticism	Putdowns	Blame
Nature of Humor	Sarcastic	Shaming	Criticizing	Demeaning	Insulting
Means of Relating	Projection	Placating	Correcting	Rescuing	Entertaining
Understanding Others	Understands Onlies; understood by Onlies	Understands First Borns; understood by First, Second, Third, and Fourth Borns	Understands First and Second Borns; understood by Third and Fourth Borns	Understands First, Second, Third Borns; understood by Third and Fourth Borns	Understands First, Second, and Third Borns; understood by Fourth Borns
Spirituality	Ethical, telling the story	Relational, the loving community	Disciplinary, sacrifice to save others	Devotional, strength through prayer	Mystical, encounter with God

Birth Order Matrix: Miscellaneous

	Only Child	First Born	Second Born	Third Born	Fourth Born
Extrovert/Introvert	Introvert	Extrovert	Introvert	Extrovert	Introvert at home, extrovert away
Expression of Love	Worry	Agreement	Constructive criticism	Pleasing	Giving
Driving Style	Drive confidently, trusting other drivers	Drives cautiously, as if others are out to get him/her	Drives angrily, because others violate rules	Drives fearfully or fearlessly	Drives slowly, watching surroundings, or recklessly
Listening Style	Puts own meaning in others' words	Listens only to others, not to self	Listens for mistakes	Interprets the intent behind what is said	Listens to others or self, but not simultaneously
Common Sayings	"You know"	"I don't know"	"You need to . . ."	"No problem"	"Try hard"
Responds To	"I don't know about you, but . . ."	"You may not agree with this, but . . ."	"This may not be perfect, but . . ."	"Please . . ."	"This may be hard for you to believe, but . . ."
Effective Confrontations	"You can be angry if you want, but . . ."	"I want you to . . ."	"Do you have any other criticisms?"	"I'm disappointed that you . . ."	"Stop it! It's like this . . ."

Birth Order Matrix: Positive Attributes

	Only Child	First Born	Second Born	Third Born	Fourth Born
Careers	Radio, finance, teaching, management: time, space, and things	Business, research, counseling, promotion, public speaking	Accounting, carpentry, secretarial, teaching, art, writing	Sales, police, newspaper reporting, writing, inventing, nursing	Management, teaching, comedy, dentistry, factory work
Strengths	Organization, accommodation, stability	Goal-setting, compromise, leadership	Self-discipline, determination	Emotional strength, compassion, practicality	Thinking, understanding, hard work
Parenting	Gives child space and time	Directs child toward goals	Teaches discipline, applies rules	Is protective, nurturing	Acts as a "buddy" to children
Marriage	Wants to meet partner's expectations	Goes along with partner's wishes	Puts spouse and family before self	Wants to please spouse and children	Wants to give family all they need
Friendship	Emotional, considerate	Compromising, serving	Helpful, offering constructive criticism	Close to one or two people	A loner; close friendship an exception

(continued)

Birth Order Matrix: Positive Attributes *(continued)*

	Only Child	First Born	Second Born	Third Born	Fourth Born
Work Style	Follows expert advice	Tries to impress others	Keeps things neat	Creative, ready to try new things	Hard worker, often doing things the hard way
Contributions	Organizations, self-help books	Discoveries, information, dreams	Writing, art, financial institutions	Poetry, inventions, sales	Philosophy, mysticism, renewed organizations

Birth Order Matrix: Problems

	Only Child	First Born	Second Born	Third Born	Fourth Born
Relational	Feels other's feelings; is a fixer	Fears others may be offended; is a placater	Is sensitive to others' anger; is a peacemaker	Is sensitive to other's wants/needs; is a pleaser	Feels trapped by other's feelings; is a controller
Sense of Shame	For appearing self-centered	For appearing guilty	For making mistakes	For appearing fearful	For appearing immature
The Child Within	Smothered	Abandoned	Neglected	Wounded	Isolated
Procrastination	Puts off big tasks while doing small tasks	Puts things off while dreaming of accomplishing things	Puts things off until they can be done perfectly	Puts things off to pursue more interesting tasks	Puts things off because others want them done
Blind Spot	What others think/feel	What he/she wants, thinks, feels	Others' emotions	Working with others	Trusting others
Boundaries	Recognizes boundaries for self and others	Perceives others as being unreachable	Strict boundaries, defined by rules	Cannot set boundaries for others	Strict boundaries for self, not allowed for others
Walk in the Woods	Stays on the path	Picks distant goals, encounters many difficulties	Watches ground, goes around in circles	Only goes into the woods to help others	Does not go in, but tells others where to go and how to get there

All animals except man know that
the ultimate of life is to enjoy it.
—Samuel Butler

Chapter Four

Opening Your Mind to the Possibilities of Birth Order

You should be feeling pretty good right now. This journey of self-exploration is meant only to be a positive experience. Of course, that doesn't mean that a little stretching and searching and serious seeking isn't going to give you a few aches and pains—but they should be the good kind of pains. You know, the ones that hurt just a little bit and that you know are making you better and stronger and healthier. That is what *The Birth Order Effect* is supposed to be teaching you—how to be a stronger and healthier person. So, if you have a dull ache anywhere inside or outside of your body then congratulations!

Before we take a look at each individual Birth Order Personality, it's important to understand how Birth Order Personality actually develops. It's not something that was shot into your arm the day after your mother gave birth to you, and it's not entirely something your mother or your father passed along via genetics.

Birth Order Personality develops out of something even more interesting than all the things we already know. The specific Personalities develop as coping strategies each one of us used as children to make ourselves feel okay in our particular positions in the family. Think about this: A second-born child is surely going to act differently than the first-born, even if they both have the same hair, the family gap between their two front teeth, and big feet.

As a family grows, each child develops his or her own coping strategies depending on their position in the family. We have already determined that those positions are limited to an Only Child, or First, Second, Third, or Fourth Born. The coping strategies they display may be to please, to be perfect, to be strong, to try hard, or to hurry, depending on their position in the family.

Since Birth Order is made up of coping skills, the nature of the home life determines the intensity of Birth Order Personality. The more harmonious the home, the less coping is necessary and the more benign the Birth Order Personality. In families where children must cope with abuse, neglect, substance abuse, chaos, overprotection, unreasonable control, frequent punishment, and unreasonable demands, they develop very strong Birth Order characteristics. Since these children become the adults seen in counseling, Birth Order effects can be more clearly observed in them than in the general population.

Here's the deal, and it's one that worrisome parents will love, especially if they think that some minor mistake they made may have ruined a child's life (consider it an early Christmas present from *The Birth Order Effect*). *Children develop Birth Order strategies for coping with siblings rather than in response to their parents*. Really. The thousands of clients who have passed through Cliff Isaacson's counseling doors have proven this to be true time and time again. Of course, any traumatic or terrible family situation will have an effect on children just as a positive and supportive family experience will remain inside of them. But Birth Order Personalities, the particular ins and outs of each one of us, develop as a result of our interactions with our brothers and sisters.

At what point can a child learn about Birth Order? It can be learned as early as four years of age. Younger siblings in a family can understand Birth Order more readily than the First or even Second Born. When the First Born puzzles over the behavior of the younger siblings, he or she is ready to consider Birth Order. The Second Born may show an interest in Birth Order when he or she is old enough to be interested in being perfect, and not because he or she is trying to understand others. Third and Fourth Borns are trying to understand how to deal with older siblings who can overpower them, so they take to understanding Birth Order early.

Gender does not enter into the development of Birth Order because Birth Order Personalities are established so early in life. When the oldest child becomes a First Born through loss of love to the new baby, it does not matter what the baby's gender is. For the Second through the Fourth Born, the gender of the older sibling makes no difference because it takes the same strategies to cope with an older brother or sister at age two or so, when the Birth Order Personality is developed.

Interestingly enough, every child can be the same Birth Order Personality if it is Only Child. One family had six Only Children because whenever a baby was born, a member of the extended family who was a nun came in to help the mother. Having done this each time a baby was born, she kept the older one from losing attention to the baby. Having all Only Children can make for a chaotic household as they all struggle against intrusion, express their feelings loudly, and throw their tantrums.

The Development of Birth Order Personality Characteristics

Here are some general rules of thumb that will help you sort through this entire process of understanding yourself through Birth Order Personality.

1. Except for the First Born and Only Child, children develop Birth Order characteristics by coping with the next older child.
2. The Only Child has to deal with being by him- or herself.
3. The First Born must cope with the loss of attention to the Second Born.
4. The Second Born must constantly cope with the attention-seeking First Born.
5. The Third Born must cope with a perfectionist Second Born.
6. The Fourth Born must cope with a strong-willed Third Born.

Out of these unique relationships each child will then develop his or her own Birth Order characteristics. See, and you thought it would be easier if you could only have been the first-born. Think again. It was a jungle growing up, for all of us. But jungles are lots of fun if you have the right equipment. The challenges and pleasures of being in a family, learning how to cope, and, most important, learning how to survive are lessons that are now part of all of us and lessons that have helped us become adults.

The dynamics of a family, especially the ways in which children relate to each other, has an overwhelming effect on our personality. Ask any adult right now about something he or she remembers learning from an older or younger sibling, and you will unearth dozens of stories.

Researchers throughout the world have determined in study after study that the early years of a child's life are the most important. Children are like little sponges; they soak up actions, thoughts, and relationships as if they were dying of thirst. This is just as true when it comes to Birth Order Personality. Although it's fairly impossible to remember what it was like when we were one and two years old, what did happen and how we reacted to it has really set the pace for our entire lives.

Just so you know, in case you have the phone in your hand and are getting ready to call the older brother who used to torture you so you can say, "See, I told you you would ruin my life by being so rotten to me when we were kids," try to remember that he didn't have it any easier. Also, remember that once you turn into an adult, you are supposed to be able to figure out how to behave, act, react, and deal with whatever negative bits and pieces of your life that might need a bit of fixing.

> "To love oneself is the beginning of a lifelong romance."
>
> —Oscar Wilde

Birth Order Personality offers you the chance to do just that. Remember and know in your heart that the formation of your Birth Order Personality was a natural and normal series of events. If you are a Fourth Born, it was not wrong or bad for you to have to figure out how to cope with your strong-willed Third Born sibling. You did what you had to do, and those Personality traits that you developed in the process have made you the unique and charming individual you are today.

If you take some time to think about your growing-up

years, some of these coping mechanisms will leap right to
the front of your mind. There are millions of First Born men
and women walking around who can still feel the sting of
what they perceived as the loss of their parents' affection to
that newborn baby.

One twelve-year-old boy remembers vividly how he felt
after the birth of his baby sister. "It was great at first, but
then, even though I was a little boy, I remember feeling really
bad because she was getting all the attention," he said. "One
day I just couldn't take it anymore and I smacked her right
in the face." The boy tears up a bit just remembering this,
because—as you might guess—the response from his sister
was pretty immediate, and the response from his mother was
right behind that of his little sister. "I still feel terrible about
it, and I know she can't remember it, but I still think about
it and it makes me sad."

That wasn't the end of the boy's bad days with his sister.
His mother remembers how many times she had to reassure
the boy that he was still loved over the next ten years. He
would occasionally come to her and say, "Mom, do you love
her more than you love me?" or "I wish she would go away
so I could have you all to myself."

The wise mother always had a positive response. "Oh,
honey," she would say, "Both your daddy and I love you in
a very special way. We have a special way to love you and
a special way to love your sister. One way is not better than
the other way."

Once this mother realized how her son felt—that he
often thought he wasn't loved and that his sister received
special treatment—she made extra efforts to let him know he
could never be replaced. She also did her best to make certain that her son had quality time alone with both her and
her husband.

In an all-out moment of pure bravery, the boy admitted
that he still feels bad sometimes when the sister is the

center of attention. "It seems stupid now, because my parents love us both so much and my sister and I are very close, but once in a while I get that old feeling and it still gets to me."

This First Born boy has not only been blessed with a great set of parents and a sister who is his best friend, but he is also able to understand how a First Born often feels and reacts. That understanding will continue to help him as he grows into adulthood and can see himself as a positive influence in his sister's and parents' life. His relationship with his sister has helped him to develop his Birth Order Personality and continues to do so.

It is important to remember that chronological birth order does not always determine a child's Birth Order Personality, although the majority of men and women actually do have the same chronological birth order and Birth Order Personality. For example, an only child often has an Only Child Birth Order Personality, a chronological first-born often has a First Born Birth Order Personality, and so forth. There are some exceptions, especially because of the role played by secondary characteristics. However, most of us have a Birth Order Personality that reflects our chronological birth order.

Exceptions to Birth Order Personality

Here are some of the rules that deal with exceptions to Birth Order Personality:

1. *With the exception of Onlies, Birth Order Personality is set by age two.* It cannot be changed after that period. There is no way to camouflage or to cover up a Birth Order Personality that, for some strange reason, we may not like (remember, there are no bad ones)—no big cloth

to drape over yourself like a magician. This is it; if you are an Only Child or a First, Second, Third, or Fourth Born Personality, that's what you are going to be for the rest of your wonderful life. Celebrate it; it is a great gift and you are one of a kind.

2. *If there are five or more years between the first and second child, the Birth Order will start over, with the first-born remaining an Only Child and the second child also being an Only Child—unless there is a third-born, who will cause the second-born to become a First Born Personality.* The reasons for this seemingly complicated exception is that a first-born child who is five years old or older at the time of the birth of the second child does not conclude that a mother's love is lost because Mother is taking care of the new baby. An older child will use reason rather than reacting emotionally to the situation, as a younger child would.

    This might be an easy exception to comprehend if you think of a family—maybe even your own—where the mother had a second child years after the first child was born. The older, more mature child usually welcomes the baby into the family like a new friend.

3. *If a mother has help in the house preventing the first-born from losing attention to the new baby, the first-born will retain his or her Only Child Birth Order personality.* This often happens if a grandmother or aunt or close friend comes in to spend time with the first-born while the new baby is being introduced into the family. If the first-born has an opportunity like this to get used to the baby and feel that the baby is part of the family and also entitled to the mother's love, this child will not feel unloved as the result of discovering that the mother also loves the baby. This child will then maintain his or her Only Child Birth Order Personality.

4. *A third-born will have a Third Born Personality even*

if there are as many as fourteen years between the second-born and third-born. Even with a large difference in age, the Second Born Personality can pick on the third-born mercilessly, creating the Third Born Personality. It's no secret that a fifteen-year-old can torment a one-year-old sibling, especially if the parents are not around to catch it. Watch the neighborhood kids for a while and you will see this happen in a matter of moments. You might even remember it happening to you if you have older siblings or did it yourself (hey, we're all naughty once in a while). Some things you never forget, but try to remember that forgiveness is a good thing.

5. *A fourth-born will be a Fourth Born Personality even if there are as many as ten years between the fourth- and third-born.* This may sound familiar to some of you. A Third Born Personality can make a sibling ten years younger feel immature and unwanted, thus creating the Fourth Born Personality.

6. *Twins organize themselves into consecutive Birth Order Personalities.* It does not seem to matter which twin was born first. One of them may become a Second and the other a Third or one will become a First and the other a Second or—well, get the picture? If Mom went wild and had triplets, or more than triplets, the same rule applies (except that this mom would be a saint).

7. *If the mother is a Third Born Personality, she could determine the Birth Order Personality of the oldest child, making a boy into a Third Born Personality or a girl into a Fourth Born Personality.* (This gender-based distinction will be explained in detail in Chapter 10.) The other siblings would then follow in order.

Third Born Personality mothers find parenting to be stressful because they are trying to control their children by pleasing them. This is really a difficult way to parent;

it creates way too much stress in the family and really brings out the Third Born Personality of the mother so that she ends up causing the oldest child to toe the line and follow her own Birth Order Personality.

This is another specific scenario where it is helpful to think of a family you know who may have a mother like this; perhaps your own mother or a mother-in-law was like this. Think about the parenting style; think about the oldest child and see if this description doesn't fit. We've all seen these moms and heard them say things to their children like, "Honey, don't do that again. Here's a piece of candy."

8. *Although day care situations do not seem to create Birth Order Personalities, other exceptions to these rules can occur when a child is two or younger and spends time with a day care provider's children.*

9. *A child who dies may or may not affect the other children's Birth Order Personalities.* Specialists need to look at individual situations to determine if that deceased child counts in the family's Birth Order Personality makeup.

10. *Birth Order is recycled in larger families.* When the fifth child comes on the scene the Fourth Born ignores him, hoping with all her heart to be able to pass on the feeling of being unwanted. So the Fourth Born does not respond to the fifth child, does not play with the fifth child, or interact with him. Without interaction with the Fourth Born the fifth child, by default, develops the personality of an Only Child. If there is a sixth child, the fifth child can feel the loss of love to the baby and thus become a First Born. In large families Birth Order can repeat from First through Fourth more than once.

If grandmother or other caretaker shows up on the scene when the sixth child is born, the fifth can develop the Only Child Personality. In one family, the ninth child, who followed two cycles of First through Fourth Born in a family of seventeen children, developed the personality of an Only Child. When her younger sibling, i.e., the tenth child, was born, mother had help from a young woman who moved in for a time. This allowed the ninth child to remain an Only Child. Her next younger sibling became a First Born followed by a Second Born and so on through the Birth Order personalities.

Siblings do not prevent the recycling of Birth Order in a family. You might think that older children would take care of the fifth child so that there would not be loss of love to the sixth child, but this does not happen. The older children are more interested in the baby than they are the fifth child and so this child may feel the loss of love even more acutely.

Often the Fourth Born and the following Only Child get along well as they get older. That does not affect the Birth Order of the Only Child.

11. *In harmonious families the Birth Order of children can be quite mild.* They do not have to develop the coping strategies they might have needed in more dysfunctional families. The Only Child does not have to struggle with intrusion because he or she is given the time to play alone. The First Born gets attention as well as the younger siblings. The Second Born gets recognized for his or her accomplishments, the Third Born is made to feel safe and the Fourth Born is included in family discussions. The patterns of Birth Order personality are still there but they do not cause problems.

These rules can really help you think about your own Birth Order Personality and the Personalities of the people you deal with. It might also help you to know that people who are using this unique concept of understanding often grasp it after lots of study and some pretty serious thinking.

Understanding Birth Order Personality

Understanding the details of Birth Order Personality doesn't just happen overnight. You will probably need to read sections of *The Birth Order Effect* several times before the light suddenly goes on, and you think, "Oh, now I get it!"

> "Genius, in truth, means little more than the faculty of perceiving in an unhabitual way."
>
> —William James

That's how understanding Birth Order Personality seems to work with the majority of people.

One day you could be having a conversation, and someone might say something that really gives away their Birth Order Personality. If you ask them about their chronological birth order, you will probably find that it corresponds to what you guessed about their Birth Order Personality. This will give you some quick insights into that person's personality, and just like that, you will see how *The Birth Order Effect* has changed your life.

Thinking in a new way is not easy. It really is true that it's hard to teach an old dog a new trick, but it's not impossible. With Grandpa John Glenn flying around in space, great-grandmothers running marathons, and the ever-expanding potential of the human brain, there really isn't anything we can't do.

If you have always thought about yourself in a specific way, this is your chance to see yourself, and others, as having great potential.

Cliff Isaacson has stressed through his many years of counseling that understanding Birth Order Personality is a totally positive experience. He believes that if people can step outside of themselves for a minute and see how their Personality was formed, it will explain a great many things to them.

It also offers people who want to change great hope.

Those with strong Birth Order Personalities may want to stop lashing out, to start working on relationships, to be able to smile in the rain. Anything becomes possible if we can see ourselves as a distinct Personality that can go anywhere and do anything. Remember, though: You can never change your Birth Order Personality. If you are an Only Child, First, Second, Third, or Fourth Born, that's what you are going to always be. But what you can understand you can learn from. Once you know your Birth Order Personality, you can make adjustments to your behavior and react to things in ways you never thought possible. You can adopt new and positive strategies for success in friendships, marriage, and your professional life.

Knowing people's Birth Order Personality enables you to interpret correctly what they are saying. You know how to interpret an Only's words by putting them in the right context. You learn to express your own opinion first when talking with a First Born. You can avoid feeling hurt at suggestions from a Second Born as you realize this person wants to help you achieve perfection rather than find fault with you. You can avoid taking the comparisons of a Third Born as putdowns and treat them as interesting ways to make connections. You can enjoy repartee with the analytical Fourth Born who might approach a subject from unusual angles.

You establish rapport with people as you reflect their Birth Order characteristics to them. Watch the Only light up when you remark on her being organized, the First Born when you tell him you like his goals, the Second Born on your observation that she pays attention to details, the Third Born as you comment on his creativity, and the Fourth Born as you notice how well she thinks things through. Everyone likes to be understood by someone else.

Birth Order Personality gives people a way to understand behaviors that might otherwise seem more than confusing.

Birth Order Personality really can be a road map into the sometime puzzling world of human behavior.

Here's one fascinating Birth Order Personality lesson that can be learned about getting things done.

Lesson from the Only Child: Get organized. That means setting a starting time and an ending time for doing something. You are more apt to get things done when you have a time for doing it.

Lesson from the First Born: Get others' thoughts. You cannot think of everything yourself. Listening to others gives you a head start.

Lesson from the Second Born: Pay attention to details. Rather than being overwhelmed by the big picture, just look at all the details of the job. As you examine details you become aware of what you can do.

Lesson from the Third Born: Compare. Compare whatever you are dealing with to something else. The comparison will generate new ideas for you.

Lesson from the Fourth Born: Analyze. In dealing with an issue, ask yourself "what if" questions to expand the realm of possibility. The "what if" questions will stimulate your subconscious with new possibilities that may occur to you at any time.

Now doesn't all that sound pretty darn positive? It is! So is thinking about and learning about Birth Order Personality. It's really no different from the half-empty/half-full life philosophy. With Birth Order Personality, your cup definitely runneth over with knowledge and understanding that can only enhance your own life and the lives of the people with whom you interact.

The adventure for you is just beginning, and it's going to continue to be exciting. The following chapters detail each of the five Birth Order Personalities, beginning with the Only Child (and what a Personality that is!).

If some of the Personality traits described in the following chapters seem negative to you, try not to see every characteristic in yourself because odds are you don't have them all. The way you express your Personality is unique. That is what makes Birth Order Personality so engaging. We are all unique and individual; we are not perfect and we are not expected to be. Remember also that the power of suggestion does exist, which is why we have tried to thoroughly explain all the Birth Order Personality traits.

Describing why certain Birth Order characteristics develop helps to define the dynamics of those characteristics. A feeling of inadequacy, for example, could be based in the experience of having had an older sibling take attention away from you. Turning the focus from what you are like as a person to the life experiences that made you that way makes it clear that you do not have to take the description of the characteristics personally, as if there were something wrong with you.

Understanding Birth Order Personality can be a totally liberating experience. This look at yourself and your personality offers a diagnosis, not a prescription. Birth Order is not identified so we can say, "You are an Only Child and you have to live with it." That's not the point at all. The message really is, "This is the pattern you have been living. This is how you can transcend it."

It's a positive, simple approach to making your own life better. Understanding yourself will provide you with the ability to make the most of your experiences and your relationships.

If you had really listened the first time, you
might have heard what I meant to say.
—Unknown Only Child

Chapter Five

Leave Me Alone;
I'd Rather Do It Myself:
The Only Child

If you happen to be reading this in a waiting room, at a mall,
or on a train, stop for just a minute and take a look around
you. See anybody with a time organizer in their hands? Are
they writing down what they are going to do next? Sneak
over and take a look. If they are writing like crazy, guess
what? You are looking at an Only Child.

Here's a list of Only Child characteristics to get you
started. If you find yourself in here somewhere, you have an
Only Child Birth Order Personality.

Only Child Birth Order
Personality Characteristics

- You wake in the morning with a schedule for the
  day in mind.

- You talk time ("It's time for you to . . .").
- You feel frustrated when things do not go well.
- You worry when there is no need to worry.
- You feel pressured.
- You need to have time to yourself—you crave it, and you have to have it.
- You don't like to be corrected, but you can shrug off criticism.
- You solve problems by getting organized.
- You don't say what you mean but something close to it.
- You have to be fair by giving equally.
- You like to stay up late and get up late.
- You make "to do" lists and cross things off rather than check them off.
- You have to do everything on your lists.
- You do little jobs first, big jobs later.
- You don't like being interrupted.

Is this you? Welcome home, Mr. or Ms. Only Child. Keep on going; it only gets better.

Like all of the Birth Order Personalities, Onlies have many fascinating and diverse traits that make them unique. Because of individual family dynamics, the Only Child Birth Order Personality is the most common personality. One out of every four people is an Only Child.

A large number of Onlies come from families in which the mother had live-in help after having subsequent children and from multigenerational families who live together. That's because someone was there to reassure them and to let them know that they were still loved, even though there were more people in the family taking up Mom and Dad's time.

If you are an Only Child, think you are an Only Child, or deal with the millions of men, women, and children who are Onlies, then you'd better sit up and pay attention. Actually, that's something an Only Child would say. Onlies, by the way, would be really frustrated if they had to read about all the other Birth Orders first. That's why, even though Onlies can appear anywhere in a family, they are making their grand appearance at the head of the line here. There are so many Onlies out there, we need to keep them all happy.

Remember that an Only Child can be found in the middle of a family, at the end, or at the beginning, in addition to being the only child in the family. In large families, the first one or two children can both be Onlies. Isaacson has discovered that the youngest child in a family of five, nine, or thirteen children will also be an Only Child if there are no other exceptions to Birth Order.

There is probably not a person alive who at one time or another did not say, "I wish I was an only child." For most of us the next sentence, if we happened to be talking to a sibling at the time, would have been, "By the way, I hate your guts." Shame on us! It's not a picnic being an only child, and being an Only Child psychologically, as with all the Birth Order Personalities, has it ups and downs as well.

Here is a list of Only Child traits. Remember, you will not have all of these characteristics, but at least five of them will fit you if you are an Only Child. If you can check off at least that many, then welcome to the club.

Only Child Personality Traits

- Is an organizer
- Is a scheduler
- Is an emotional worrier
- Is a reactionary
- Is dependable
- Feels pressured
- Needs time alone

- Interrupts
- Projects thoughts, feelings, and motives onto others
- Tries to avoid feeling disappointed
- Practices equal justice
- Expects others to be fair
- Throws tantrums to exercise power
- Makes lists
- Dislikes intrusion
- Displays a sarcastic type of humor

There you have it, a list for Onlies. That wasn't so bad, was it? Now you can say to your baby brother, "Well, at least I'm not a Third Born." Of course, he'll say, "Well, it's better than being an Only Child." A terrific example of an Only Child is Oprah Winfrey. Now, here's a woman who has got it together. She relates well to herself and is a terrific example of someone who is honest and practices what she preaches. Her feelings are reflected in her facial expressions and body language. I bet if she were to let us sneak into her office we would find that it is littered with lists and lots of pens to cross off all the things she must accomplish each day. Keep her in mind if you need an example of a real-life Only Child.

Right off the bat, the poor Onlies begin life having to deal with two major problems. First of all, they have to figure out how they can play alone without feeling lonely. The second question they constantly ask themselves is, "What can I do about all the interference in my life?" First, let's deal with the Onlies' answer to problem number one.

How the Only Child Copes with Feelings of Loneliness

To keep from being lonely, the Only Child quickly develops imaginary friends. One little boy in Wisconsin had a great little pal he called Sarchey. His mother discovered Sarchey one day as she walked by her son's bedroom and saw him holding open the closet door and talking.

"What are you doing, sweetie?" she asked him.

"Playing," he responded.

"Who are you playing with?"

"With my friend Sarchey. Don't you know Sarchey?" he asked, genuinely shocked that his mother didn't know this important person in his life.

The mother kept cool. She got down on her knees and asked him what Sarchey looked like.

"He's just a little person, Mom. Somebody to play with me."

"Okay, then," said his mother. "You behave in here and see if he wants to stay for dinner."

"Mom, he lives here. Of course he'll stay for dinner."

Sarchey lived with this family for a long time. He slept in this little boy's bed, went to church with the family, but when the little boy went to preschool, Sarchey had to stay home. This family still laughs about the time they were on a family vacation and the boy started yelling for his father to pull over.

"What is it?" asked the concerned father who pulled the car over immediately.

"Sarchey has to go to the bathroom."

Now, there's a creative little Only Child who came up with a terrific way of dealing with his loneliness. He spent many happy hours with Sarchey and had a great life until his sister was born—but that's a story for another chapter.

Onlies don't just have imaginary friends to keep them company. Their friend can be a special toy, a pet, or even a parent if the parent allows the child to do this. To the Only Child this is all serious business. As with Sarchey, these imaginary friends develop distinct identities, attitudes, and directions for behaviors. This imaginary friend feels what the Only Child projects, thinks what the Only Child wants him or her to think, and does what the Only Child thinks he or she should do. As you may have guessed, when Sarchey had to go to the bathroom so did the little boy. Well, it is kind of cute, isn't it?

This imaginary friend business turns into serious work as Onlies grow up and turn into Only Child adults. Onlies never seem to let go of their love for this imaginary section of their life. See if this sounds familiar: Do you or does someone you know think of his or her car as part of the family? A close friend? Something he or she can talk to? Do you know anyone who has actually named their car? The blue truck becomes Big Blue. The red convertible becomes Stella. These Onlies don't wash their cars. They give them baths. They think the cars will feel bad if they were dirty—and would feel worse if they were ever sold. Onlies often shed tears when they have to sell these precious automobiles. They may take photos of them and display the photos in a special place, or call to find out who purchased the car so they can see how it's doing.

These types of attachments do not just extend to cars, trucks, tractors, snowmobiles, or lawn mowers. Onlies turn special objects at home into friends as well—whether it's an old footstool, the blue drinking glass he's had since high school, the old doorknob from the first apartment, or the basketball jersey with his favorite number on it from fourth grade. Onlies love their things and love to be at home, alone, surrounded by them. Sometimes Onlies stay up after everyone else has gone to bed or they get up before everyone else does in order to have time alone to enjoy the company of their imaginary friends—even if the friend is an old coaster or the television set.

It would come as no big revelation that sending an Only Child to his or her room is not punishment but a great reward. Only Children love to be alone, when they can play with all their imaginary friends and not be bothered. This alone time energizes them, and when they are told they can come out of their room, they are really happy and the parents think the punishment worked. Ha! The Only Child had a ball.

Parents who think this type of punishment didn't work are both right and wrong. A better punishment might be to make the child play with a whole group of children for hours and hours on end. Actually, if the end result is to change a child's attitude, then sending him or her to their room would help. The child would end up happy, as would the parents for getting a bit of a break.

These cool Onlies often look at real flesh-and-blood friends as imaginary also. As a result, they may tend to interrupt their friends frequently, because they think they already know what they are thinking and so don't need to hear what they have to say.

When friends have problems, Onlies give advice freely and think the advice is perfect. They expect their friends to act on the advice, just as their imaginary friends had done whatever they suggested. That's why so many self-help books are authored by Onlies. Onlies who think they can innately understand problems also feel that if more people could just get a piece of their good advice, there would be lots more happy people in the world. Hey, some of the books are pretty good—especially this one.

If you take a look at some of these self-help books you might notice that many of these authors think that everyone in the world is in dire need of privacy. This, of course, is a pretty big need for the Only Child, and Onlies often do not realize that privacy is not an issue for others. Most of us like a little privacy when we need it, but we sure don't need it like the Only Child does.

Many of the Only Child–written self-help books deal with issues that are near and dear to an Only Child heart. Time management, getting to do what you want, coping with pressure, taking control of your life, how to feel good, how to get your children to do what you want, how to juggle work and home life, and how to organize your house are all perfect Only Child themes.

Missing from this list are other Birth Order concerns, such as coping with people who put you down, dealing with panic or anxiety, being overlooked for promotions, overcoming depression, inability to focus, detachment from feelings, psychological self-defense, and rejection. Popular books that deal with non–Only Child issues will almost always be authored by a Birth Order Personality other than an Only Child, and those authors almost always write about their own Birth Order issues. Thank heavens they do; we all need help.

When Onlies stop and think about others and relationships, they tend to put themselves in others' situations. If an Only Child husband needs to understand something about his wife, for example, he will try and imagine how she feels. He would say to himself, "Well, that's how she must feel." This practice is a result of the tendency of Onlies to treat others as the product of their imaginations.

What the wife would like is to have her husband treat her as an individual with her own feelings, attitudes, and reactions—to realize that it's impossible for the husband to slip inside of her mind because she is real, not imaginary. Once the Only Child husband understands this, he will have a more positive experience with his wife or with anyone he interacts with.

On the flip side, an Only Child often takes on the feelings of others in a symbiotic relationship. If someone feels bad, the Only Child feels bad. If someone is happy, you can count on the Only Child to be happy, also. Remember your Mom asking you if you would jump off the pier if someone else did? Well, the Only Child actually would have jumped. It's very important for Onlies to know that others feel good for them to feel good themselves. That's why Onlies will go out of their way to make sure everyone is happy. Then they can be happy too.

Many people who deal with Onlies catch on to this after a while and begin keeping their emotions in check. They know that once they reveal themselves, the Only Child will work hard to do whatever he or she can to change how they feel. This isn't necessarily a bad thing, but some people just want to stay in control of how they feel.

People are not always offended by Onlies treating them as if they were imaginary, because not everyone realizes they are doing it. Lots of people take what the Onlies have to say as something positive that can help them. It's all good news to them. They may internalize the information and make a resolution to try and live up to it. Yet the Only will just continue as usual, never realizing how his or her behavior has affected others.

One woman in a large city made some life-changing decisions once she realized that even though she has a sister, she has an Only Child Birth Order Personality. She was experiencing problems in her marriage because she felt as if she and her husband, whom she loved, were not connecting.

Her husband held a full-time job and was also very active in a hobby that kept him away from home for hours many evenings. This woman loved it when her husband was gone, because it gave her some of that alone time she craved. She enjoyed getting the kids ready for bed on her own, and organizing things around the house her own way. The woman said that when her husband was home, she felt "smothered" and unable to do the things she wanted, even though her husband never attempted to keep her from doing so.

This man had the habit of simply plopping down in front of the television set when he was home and ignoring his wife and children—until their youngest son, a Second Born, learned to stand in front of the television set and block his father's view. Once the man realized what he had been doing, he became a terrific dad.

It was pretty obvious to an outside viewer that this woman and her husband were living in two separate worlds. Once the woman found out that her husband was also an Only Child who had the same needs and desires she did, she became more content with the relationship. She even began to imagine how painful life with someone of a different Birth Order Personality might have been. Someone with another Birth Order Personality might have made more demands on her and her time. Under those circumstances she might have lost some control over her life and not had the time alone that she needed to survive. For an Only Child, it's not so bad to have the other partner be in their own world, too, and to be able to make contact with him or her only when you want to.

This woman drastically changed the quality of her life, and probably of her husband's life, by gaining an understanding of what she needed and what her husband needed. This is an example of the positive results of using Birth Order—how it can benefit you and the people you live with.

Even siblings in a family with Onlies do not understand them. Onlies do not manipulate or overpower others, and they don't need the other siblings to understand them. And because the other siblings do not try to manipulate or overpower the Onlies, they don't need to understand them either. Thus, even their siblings do not know how an Only Child's mind works.

Stay calm, this isn't bad. Onlies, you are precious and wonderful. Onlies develop a keen sense of drama from those imaginary relationships and that's very appealing. Onlies are natural storytellers who can put feeling and action into their stories. Could anything be better? If you are not an Only Child you will surely recognize this trait in someone you know—or perhaps even in someone you sit across from at the table each evening.

An Only Child will read a story to his or her children and make the clock stand still. The kids will listen as if they have been transported back to Cinderella's front steps. Now, if this isn't a gift, what is? I bet many of use would love someone to read us a story like that right now, even if we are supposed to be all grown up.

Their talent for speaking causes many Onlies to go into the radio business. They make wonderful disc jockeys, because they have that flare for drama and can relate to what seems to be a huge imaginary audience. They can converse with and entertain thousands of people at once, as if they were sitting in the control room with them. They don't need feedback; why would they? They can go on and on and on. Any of the other Birth Order Personalities would need some type of response—a list of questions, a kick in the shins. Not an Only Child. Go turn on the radio. Dozens of them are going nonstop this very moment.

The Only Child and Interruptions

Ready for some more great Birth Order Personality insights into Onlies? We are going to tackle another big issue that seems to keep Onlies preoccupied throughout their lives: how to deal with interruptions.

Here's what happens to the happily alone Only Child. When they are very young, Onlies get interrupted frequently as most small children do—either out of necessity because they are getting into something they shouldn't or simply because a parent want to spend time with them. Because much of this attention is unwanted, the Only Child then develops an aversion to intrusion. This causes the Only Child to design two speeds for keeping his or her life in motion.

Parents, take heart here before we go any further. It's perfectly fine and wonderful to want to spend time with your

Only Child and there isn't a thing you can do to keep your little Only from feeling intruded upon. As you well know, it's your job to pay attention to the little darling even if he or she doesn't want to be bothered; people who ignore their children end up in jail. This attention doesn't adversely affect an Only Child; he or she can deal with this.

As children, Onlies do things quickly to avoid intrusion. You've seen this and it can make you laugh. An Only Child will run to the toy box and take out every single toy in five seconds before someone can say, "Why don't you just take out the blocks?" This same kid will grab a green pencil and color the sky her favorite color at the speed of sound before anyone can say, "How about coloring the sky blue?"

> "If one is master of one thing and understands one thing well, one has at the same time, insight and understanding of many things."
>
> —Vincent van Gogh

Almost everyone has a sibling who did this next trick at least once. Mom steps into the living room to answer the phone and in three seconds the Only Child has spaghetti sauce up his nose, in his hair, and between his toes. These little tiger Onlies figure that if they can move really fast, no one will have time to suggest, "Why don't you . . .?"

On the other hand, when an Only Child is asked to do something that he or she does not want to do, he or she can slip into slow motion. The same Only Child who took the toys out of the toy box in five seconds will take a month to put everything back. Onlies figure that the longer they wait, the more likely it is that someone will come along and give them a hand. These Onlies are no dummies.

As Onlies turn into adults, they continue with the fast and slow speeds. They do this mentally. When an Only Child is doing chores, especially at home, he or she will be thinking about something more pleasant that he or she could be doing. Yet, believe it or not, when the Only Child is doing something fun, he or she will think about all the chores that need to be done! It's a cruel world. The result of this type of thinking is that it creates a kind of time warp in the mind of the Only Child that makes it seem as if work time expands and fun times shrink.

Only Child Birth Order Personalities often say, "All I do is work, work, work. I never get a chance to do what I want to do." When an Only Child is working, especially at home, however, he or she will steal a little time to watch television or do something hr or she finds pleasurable. Onlies will tend to put off what they have to do, and when they let themselves have some real fun, they will worry about what they didn't get done earlier.

Intrusions drive Onlies crazy. One way they deal with it is by trying hard to be master organizers. If they have structure and feel like they are in control of their home, then maybe, just maybe, others will keep out of their space, time and things.

Here's where those mighty lists and schedules come in. Onlies actually like to make lists of their lists. One woman who lives with an Only Child husband, whom she has come to understand and appreciate through the joys of Birth Order Personality Method, has taken to calling her husband's little list of everything "Daddy's life."

"It used to drive me crazy, because he writes things down when he drives, when he is eating, in the middle of a conversation," said the woman. "I started joking around with him and the kids about it, and then I realized how important this was to him." The lighthearted joking ended up leading to a series of serious conversations which resulted in the woman's understanding of an important aspect of her husband's personality.

The woman also realized that much of what her Only Child husband had written on his list were things that he wanted and felt he needed to do for his family. She embraced his list making and continues to have fun with it, but she has tried hard to get him not to write when he is driving. "I keep having this vision of this wonderful man driving us right off a cliff while he is jotting down something like, 'Be sure to check the air in all the tires.'"

In case you haven't noticed it helps to have a sense of humor no matter what Birth Order Personality you happen to be. Humor helps not only in dealing with Onlies, but in dealing with every single Birth Order.

As you might well guess, Onlies don't like it if something messes up their long and often detailed lists. Because Onlies are so organized, it drives them even further over the edge when they are interrupted. Onlies expect order. They demand it. They need it. Once they get things organized, they expect things to stay that way. If only life worked out in such a fine fashion.

When an Only Child adult has decided on a schedule of activities, for example, he or she expects to follow it to the letter. There's no way this person is going to do number three on the list before the two items preceding it have been completed. If something, or, heaven forbid, someone, inter- rupts that precious schedule, the Only Child will feel like the entire day has been "ruined."

In this case, an Only Child might feel compelled to recon- struct the entire schedule, even going so far as to rewrite the entire list if part of it has been changed. The woman men- tioned in the preceding example has seen this type of behavior in her husband hundreds of times. She has said that her husband will get a bit morose if, for example, one of her children needs to go someplace on a Saturday evening and they decide to go to church on Sunday morning instead of attending their usual Saturday evening service.

"My husband will throw a little tantrum and say that the entire day on Sunday will be ruined because we have to go to church for an hour," said the woman. "I used to think he was kidding, but then I realized that that is how he sees things."

Obviously this family can't always go to church on Saturday evening, so the woman has had to spend a great deal of time talking her husband through this challenging problem. She does admit that she tries very hard to accommodate him and that they rarely miss Saturday services, even though she doesn't much care when they go to church. For her, it isn't a big thing. For him, it is, and she accepts that.

To understand how an Only Child might feel about scheduling and organizing, picture a table full of objects. Imagine that there is no more room on the table, but something else has to be put on it. Faced with this problem, a First, Second, Third, or Fourth Born will usually take something less important off the table to accommodate the new item. An Only Child, however, would feel as if the entire table had to be completely cleared in order for a space to be found for the new item. It might seem as if the Only Child has trouble setting priorities.

Additional Only Child Attitudes and Behaviors

When it comes to raising children, Only Child parents, who solve all their problems by organizing, often give long, unwanted explanations to their children to direct their behavior. They can go on and on and on in instances where a simple explanation would have been adequate. They might find that their child will respond better if the instructions and the explanation are short and to the point.

Onlies love to influence others by offering organizational advice. One supervisor of nurses told a subordinate to just close the door to her office for an hour in order to get her paperwork done. This was after the subordinate had told her that she couldn't get any work done because the doctors kept coming in to talk with her. While this solution might seem to make sense, it didn't work in this case because the subordinate had been hired to be a liaison with the doctors.

Onlies are often much different away from home than they are at home, where they feel there are more intrusions. This difference quickly becomes apparent to an Only Child once he or she starts school. While the Only Child was the center of attention at home and was always interrupted, the teacher might have twenty-plus students, so interruptions are less likely. An Only Child does not feel the same pressures in the classroom that he or she feels at home.

Even as adults, Onlies often feel as if a weight has been lifted from their shoulders as they leave the house or apartment and feel it settle back on them when they return home. As discussed earlier, an Only Child feels more pressure if he or she is married to someone of a Birth Order Personality other than an Only Child. There can also be pressure if there are children at home, or if others, such as extended family members, are living in the home. Of course, an Only Child who lives alone doesn't feel pressure at all.

Here's a great tip for Onlies who are married to other Onlies. Go out to eat all the time. Really. If you are a true Only Child and you feel smothered at home, just head out to a restaurant where you can relax and communicate with each other away from all the stuff that interrupts you. For a spouse who would rather burn down the kitchen than cook, this is especially great advice.

One Only Child woman I know—let's call her Jean—is married to a First Born truck driver named Bob. Bob is gone all the time, driving here one week and there one week. Jean looks forward to the nights when Bob comes home, but she also looks forward to the day that he leaves.

This lucky Only Child has the best of both worlds. She

has time with her husband, and it's quality time because it's limited, but then she has plenty of alone time when he is out on the road. If he gets delayed when he is on the road, Jean is not a happy camper, and she will get angry with herself for getting angry. Likewise, if he has to leave earlier than planned, she experiences another downer. As an Only Child Jean has a need to organize her time, and part of the organization encompasses the need to know exactly when Bob will be home and when he will leave.

Onlies really tend to think with their feelings. This kind of behavior often doesn't jive with the thinking of other Birth Order Personalities, because Onlies evaluate things in terms of their own emotional responses. For example, Onlies may turn down social engagements far in advance because they don't know how they will feel when it's time to go to the party or baseball game. One man with marital problems could not determine if he wanted to stay married or get a divorce because he just didn't know how he would feel in either case. He spent a great deal of time trying to decide how he would feel so he could make a decision and get on with his life.

A special form of thinking with feelings is worry, and Onlies tend to be pretty darn good worriers. They think that if they worry, then bad things will not happen to them. A woman whose boss had to have major heart surgery felt just terrible because she had forgotten to worry about the boss when he was in the operating room. She felt that she had really let him down by not worrying.

Because they think with their feelings, Onlies may respond with temper tantrums when they get frustrated. Some Onlies may punch a wall, throw something, or shout. At times Onlies do not reason well with someone who disagrees with them. Rarely do Onlies hit someone else, unless the behavior comes from their secondary characteristics, which will be discussed in more detail in Chapter 10.

The Only Child is one Birth Order Personality that tends to take on strong secondary characteristics from parents. Yet the majority of people will always revert to primary Birth Order behavior in times of stress. So if you are trying to decide if you are an Only Child, pay attention the next time you experience a flat tire during rush hour or your child makes you late for work by being sick all over your new suit. That's a terrific way to see who you really are.

Former President Bill Clinton appears to be an Only Child Birth Order Personality. It is his Only Child Personality that has enabled him to shrug off the criticism that would have sent the rest of us into seclusion. There is a good chance that the behavior that got him in trouble and kept our newspapers full of juicy stories is a result of a combination of his Only Child Personality with Third Born Secondary characteristics.

Onlies are a fascinating and unique section of the Birth Order world. Many Onlies can come out of terrible situations and manage to get on with their lives. A young teenage girl I know proves this point. She came from an abusive family and now lives with her grandparents.

When her own parents divorced, she at first lived with her mother, who immediately got into another abusive relationship. This poor kid went from one bad scene to the next, yet she was not angry, depressed, demanding, whining, morose, or anguished.

If you met her now, you would think that she was a normal, well-adjusted teenager. This is because as an Only Child Birth Order Personality, she has the ability to retreat into her own world, which kept her mentally and emotionally intact during the hard times. Children with other Birth Order Personalities may not have been as resilient in this situation.

It did help that this girl talked about her past, and that her grandparents are providing a stable home environment. Because she had always lived in her own Only Child world, this young girl has been able to adjust to her new life and find her place in it.

There. That wasn't so bad was it? Onlies outnumber the rest of us, and they are just as interesting and challenging as the other Birth Order Personalities.

All you First Borns who have been reading this chapter and picking out your friends, mates, coworkers, and relatives get ready. It's your turn. The next chapter jumps right into the First Born Personality—and what a ride it is.

Scenery is fine—but human nature is finer.

—Keats

Chapter Six

I Don't Know;
What Do You Think?
The First Born

Here we go, First-Borns. It's been a long haul for this often-misunderstood Birth Order Personality. Old schools of thought have placed a heavy burden on your tired shoulders. Just say the word "first-born" in a crowded room and watch the response. First-borns are supposed to be strong. Leaders. Rulers of the world. After all, haven't the first-borns been heading up the family line? Not in this Birth Order. First Borns, welcome to a new world.

This Birth Order Personality has characteristics that will shatter some old assumptions about who a First Born is and how he or she should act. And remember, as with all Birth Order Personalities, the First Born can be, but does not necessarily have to be, the chronological first-born in a family.

It's time to get serious, First Borns. Here's your first chance to test yourself and see if you really are who you think you are.

First Born Birth Order Personality Characteristics

- You are goal oriented.
- You need to know what others think.
- You feel guilty when there is no reason to feel guilty.
- You worry about offending others.
- You procrastinate by daydreaming about the future.
- You feel compelled to agree with others or to have them agree with you.
- You don't understand others and you know you don't.
- You would like to impress others.
- You crave approval from people you respect.
- You cannot predict what others will do.
- You would say, "Let's do this," rather than "Do this."
- You feel superior but want to appear humble.
- You feel like you cannot get what you want.

Does any of this sound familiar? Welcome home, First Born Birth Order Personalities, and hello to anyone who wants to learn about the ins and outs of life with a First Born.

The first-born is, of course, an Only Child in the beginning. When a new baby comes along, the first-born might even remain an Only Child if he or she doesn't lose attention to the new baby. If a grandmother, favorite aunt, neighbor, or hired helper comes in to assist the new mom, there is a great chance that the chronological first-born child will remain an Only Child psychologically.

If Birth Order Personality is new to you, it may be difficult to remember at first that a First Born always starts out as an Only Child. This can be mind-boggling for someone who has spent a lifetime thinking of him- or herself as a first-born in every sense of the word. For some of you, this news may come as a relief; for others it may take some adjustment, but that's what makes life so interesting. Some wise person once said that a change is as good as a rest, and that's definitely true when it comes to learning about your Birth Order Personality.

Many parents know that a new baby in the house is going to mean lots of changes for them and for the first-born child, and that it's a good idea to prepare this child for a new brother or sister. They may include the first-born child in decisions that need to be made about the new baby: Should we give the baby your room? What color of wallpaper should we use? What do you think about this new blanket? Before the new baby is born, parents may actually increase the amount and quality of attention they give to the first-born—but until that baby makes his or her appearance, there is no way for this first-born to know what's really going to happen.

One of two things can happen next. If a mother and father are sensitive enough to the loss of love that may potentially be felt by the first-born, perhaps arranging for someone to spend time with the first-born while Mom takes care of the new sibling, this child will most likely stay as an Only Child Birth Order Personality.

If Grandma is spending hours with the first-born, talking with him, showing him what Mom is doing with the baby, and letting him know how much he is loved, the child will stay an Only Child. This is because the child does not feel the loss of the mother's love. This little guy is probably thinking something like, "Hey, the baby is cool. Grandma is playing with me. Mom still tucked me in. Life is one big bowl of sugar-coated cereal."

However, keeping tabs on two babies—even with super help—is not an easy thing to do. More often than not, the mother feels overwhelmed, or Grandma or the neighbor becomes distracted. In this case the first-born quickly becomes a First Born Birth Order Personality. This isn't a bad thing, but just how this particular Birth Order Personality develops.

It's easy to see how a young child can feel unloved when the new kid comes to town. Many adults still feel this way when they see a grown brother or sister getting something from their parents that they have never received. Be honest. You may have felt this way yourself if your mom or dad bought your sister a new car, for example, while you had to take a second job in order to buy one. It isn't easy being a grownup.

Imagine, then, how a small child feels when his or her world is suddenly shattered by the arrival of a new little prince or princess. How dreadful. How terrible. Life will never be the same. If it's hard for us big people to cope with feelings of competition with our siblings, imagine how they might make someone who comes up to our knee feel.

Right off the bat, the baby is definitely not as much fun as the first-born anticipated. It's not that all those cute folks on Sesame Street lied or anything, it's just well, who wants to share, anyway? The first-born's feelings of happy expectation, which had been encouraged by his or her parents, are soon replaced by feelings of nervousness and sadness that the baby gets all the attention.

The first-born now waits for everything. The baby is hungry. The baby has wet her diaper. The baby needs to go for a walk. The baby this and the baby that. That darn baby comes first with everyone. She's first with Mom, Dad, the neighbors who ooh and aah over her. The baby got all the gifts, the baby had her name in the paper, and all the kids at preschool want to do is talk about the baby.

This is like stepping off the edge of an invisible cliff for the first-born. One day he or she is at the center of the universe. He or she gets lots of attention, and lots of hugs and kisses—and then the new baby changes everything. This is obscene for the first-born, who thinks it is all unfair. In a matter of days, this child can go from being an Only Child Birth Order Personality to a real First Born.

Before we get back inside this new First Born's head, you might want to pause and consider some of the other Birth Order traits that make up the First Born. As with all Birth Orders, at least five of the following should fit you if you truly possess that Personality. Remember to be honest. This is no time to fool yourself or the people you love. This look at yourself is being offered to help you understand who you are and how you got that way. No one is going to make you sit in the corner. This is all good stuff.

First Born Personality Traits

- Feels guilty easily
- Is placating
- Believes justice is people getting what they deserve
- Asks questions to orient self
- Is emotionally unexpressive
- Displays a shaming type of humor
- Avoids offending others
- Daydreams about accomplishing things
- Is out of touch with self
- Is unable to connect with others
- Is a better leader than manager of people
- Is compromising
- Wants to impress

These traits are pretty revealing and interesting, don't you think? Are you ready for some more insights?

So, this new baby is in the house, and the First Born is

going crazy trying to get a handle on this new phase of life. There is more than enough time for him or her to figure this out, because all the First Born seems to be doing is waiting. Waiting for everything. In this little person's head, it's as if a big "hold" button has been turned on.

Because this First Born is just a child, he quickly begins to think that he has done something to make his mother treat him this way. The First Born does not yet know this baby, so he feels as if he has lost his mother's love to a stranger. This is a strong and lasting feeling that can stay with a strong First Born his entire life.

You can see how easily this can happen—especially if you are a First Born who has memories of a new sibling. As the First Born sits and waits for Mom to change the baby's diaper, feed the baby, and do a million other things with the baby, all she can think about is, "What did I do to make my mommy not love me anymore?" She is too young to realize that she required the same level of attention when she was a baby.

If you think that this is what happened to you, go ahead and cry if you want to. It is kind of sad, but, really, one of the joys of learning about Birth Order is understanding who you are and how you came to be that way. It's a remarkable way for each one of us to move forward in a positive fashion.

How the First Born Copes with the Loss of the Mother's Love

Those minutes and hours when a First Born child sits and waits for a parent's attention after a new baby brother or sister is born really do seem like hours. While the child is waiting, he may feel unloved and may come to the conclusion that he must earn love to be loved. As a result, love may appear to the First Born to be conditioned on his behavior. The First Born will begin to think that love is only available on a limited basis and must be earned. This is not an easy way to think about love.

First Born guilt comes from the child thinking that she has done something to make Mother not love her anymore. The First Born does not know what she might have done wrong but feels guilty, anyway. These guilty feelings can last throughout a First Born's life, arising any time the First Born believes someone is acting as if he or she does not care for the First Born.

An interesting thing happened to a First Born man whose wife went in to see a counselor so she could improve their relationship. Her counselor, someone familiar with Birth Order Personality, told the woman that she could do many things to make her First Born husband feel that he was loved. Her husband was a classic First Born who could never believe that anyone simply loved him for himself.

The wise therapist told the woman that she needed to praise her husband for something and then say to him, "But I love you because you are you."

One day the woman had her chance to try this out. Her husband had been working in the garage for weeks on a special project, and that day he rushed in and asked her to come out and see what he had done. She looked at the beautiful cabinet he had built, touched its sides, opened the doors, and ran her fingers along the fine edges he had matched up perfectly. Then she turned to her husband and said, "You did a great job building this beautiful cabinet, but I want you to know that I love you because you are you."

The husband was stunned. Tears came to his eyes and rolled down his face. His wife brushed them away and then she kissed him and went back inside. Twenty minutes later the husband came back inside, still crying, and said, "What did you do to me?"

Because First Borns have difficulty believing they are truly loved, it is important to tell them that you love them because they are "just who they are." If you just tell a First Born you love him or her, you will almost always get an "I love you, too," in return, because First Borns think that love is conditional. This is why this woman's reply worked so perfectly on her husband. By saying, "I love you because you are you," she made her husband stop and realize that he was indeed receiving unconditional love. What a great and wonderful gift this woman gave to the man she loved by understanding his Birth Order Personality.

During the days and nights when a First Born child is dealing with a new sibling, his or her future orientation also begins to develop. A First Born—or any child for that matter—will easily show sadness at not getting attention. Can you just see this? Maybe you can even remember reacting this way or watching as one of your children reacted this way. The classic pose would have the First Born child sitting outside the room where, say, Mom is changing the baby's diaper. Although she has just told her little First Born darling that she'll "be right out," that doesn't mean much to the First Born. He or she is sad and is going to make sure Mom knows about these feelings. Head in hands, with feet tucked under the legs, and maybe a few tears. We are talking major sad. Really, really sad. "Why don't you love me?" sad.

> "Poetry is not a turning loose of emotion, but an escape from emotion: it is not the expression of personality but an escape from personality."
>
> —T. S. Eliot

The First Born knows that eventually Mom will keep her word and the goofy baby will fall asleep and it will finally be his or her turn. Thus, the First Born learns to look forward to the times when his or her mother will have the time to provide the love that the First Born craves.

Let's face the facts. Sometimes the First Born throws a fit or two (or three or ten) to get attention. Most moms are smart enough to realize that this is not great behavior, and the First Born will learn that too. It feels much better to the First Born to get a "Nice job, honey," or a "You were so patient and look what a beautiful picture you drew," than a "You are a naughty child."

A wise First Born will bring his or her mother a washcloth, help tuck the baby in bed, and read a book while waiting for Mom. The reward is worth all the anxiety. Mom will cuddle the First Born in her lap, offer a cookie, and say, "Thanks for being such a big help," and this is how a First Born learns that love is earned and takes the form of approval, admiration, and respect.

First Borns will constantly look forward to things, ignoring what is present. This is what they learned from all those long minutes of waiting. It really takes just a few minutes to turn an oldest child into a First Born, because time really does go slowly for a child. The reason for this phenomenon is that we measure time according to how long we have lived.

Think about it. Time goes faster as we get older and therefore appears to be shorter. How many times have our parents told us or have we told our own children, "Wait until you get older; time will fly." Summer vacation is a good example. That slice of heaven seemed like it was going to last forever on the last day of school, and holidays seemed to take forever to get here when school started up again.

We do measure time spans by comparing how long we have lived. For example, when we are thirty years old, one year is one-thirtieth of our lifetime. However, when we were three, one year was one-third of our lifetime. So if a thirty-year-old mother takes ten minutes to change the baby's diaper, that ten minutes translates into one hundred minutes for the three-year-old, plenty of time for this small person to feel unloved.

That's why it's so tough for anyone—a grandmother, a friend, or whoever—to keep that oldest child from becoming a First Born. Someone must be there almost 100 percent of the time. Otherwise, just a few minutes transforms the Only Child into a psychological First Born. Likewise, if a mother is to keep her oldest child from becoming a First Born, she must include the child every time she gives attention to the baby.

In our experience the oldest child will remain an Only Child if Grandmother or other caretaker is there for a few days after baby comes home. It appears that after a few days, although the baby is still new to the family, the baby does not appear to be a stranger to the Only Child. The young child seems to adjust very quickly to the new baby being there. Once that happens, within three days, the Only Child is in no danger of feeling loss of love to the baby although he or she may still feel intruded on by his or her sibling for years.

Feeling unloved sounds pretty horrible, or even a bit tragic, but you Onlies, and Second, Third, and Fourth Borns, have your own problems. Stop smirking. One of you feels smothered, another feels inadequate, one of you deals with always feeling vulnerable, and another feels unwanted. You know who you are. If you don't; keep reading. The answer is in here somewhere.

Here's great news for parents everywhere: There is no way to raise a child who will not have to overcome some problems as an adult. Really. If you think of this in a positive way, you'll realize that learning how to overcome, expanding who we are and who we can become, changing, and growing are not bad but bring much of the joy of living. Sometimes parents do bad things, but how can learning and understanding and giving a child the best you have to give be bad? It can't. Maybe what some wise person said really is true: perhaps we all really do spend our entire adult lives recovering from our childhood. That may be true regardless of our Birth Order Personality, and what fun it is.

It's true that a First Born feels that love is tenuous at best. First Borns are very careful not to destroy what love they think they do have, and they could actually have a lot more than they think they do. This Birth Order Personality learns to walk on eggshells around people, is always tuned in to what the other person expects, and tries hard to meet expectations. First Borns surely don't want to lose what they do have. Consequently, a First Born is very careful about what he or she says to friends or others outside the family. Within the family, it's a different story.

First Borns are always waiting and watching to see how people outside the family will react to them to determine how they should act in turn. Should they run? Stand up and smile? Be happy? Cry? Head for the hills? If the First Born catches a glimpse of a positive response, he will sense a feeling of relief. If, on the other hand, the First Born senses a negative response, he will feel guilty at offending the other person, even if he has done nothing wrong and has just completely misjudged the other person's reaction. The First Born will jump to the conclusion that he has ruined the possibility of having any type of relationship with this person.

If a total stranger happens to smirk at a First Born as he walks by, the First Born will feel as if someone has smacked him upside the head. He will take this random gesture as a personal attack. Let's say a First Born is bold enough to try and find a parking space in downtown Chicago. After finding a space, he pulls in and then glances in the rearview mirror to see that someone else had his eye on the parking spot. The First Born will immediately feel guilty for having offended this person. The First Born's reaction in these types of situations does not have to have any connection with reality. Rather, it stems from that early experience of feeling guilty for losing mother's love.

While all this worry and angst about loss of love is going on, it's easy to see how a First Born might lose track of her own feelings. The focus for a First Born is always on someone else's needs, wishes, and wants. If you ask a First Born about her needs and wants, the response will be an automatic "I don't know." Sometimes the First Born does know what she wants but will not take the risk of revealing it without first trying to find out what the other person's attitude toward her might be.

First Born telemarketers can overcome the First Born's difficulties with self-expression because they have to talk fluently on the phone. Yet they still interrupt themselves. Most First Borns use "word whiskers" like, "uh," "er," and "um," or they pause or grunt because they don't know what to say next.

First Borns have the most trouble when they don't get feedback, because they depend on knowing what someone else thinks. Just listen to a radio talk show for a while and you can pick out the First Borns immediately. They do not know what to say unless the host says something to them. What the host does say will suggest the direction they take. Onlies, on the other hand, always know what to say in such situations and hardly pay attention to what the talk show host has to say.

First Borns can easily bore others because they never seem to have an opinion of their own. They appear noncommittal or overly agreeable. The First Born does not like to express anything controversial. Yet, First Borns do like to talk about things that they expect to achieve. This often gives the impression that they are trying to impress their listener and makes that person feel uncomfortable. So the poor First Born, who is searching around for some kind of lasting relationship, can end up being his or her own worst enemy.

A minister who learned about Birth Order Personality quickly discovered that he had a First Born Birth Order

Personality. When this man learned that First Borns often talk about what they hope to achieve, what great and lofty goals they have, or what wonders they may have already accomplished, he stopped and took a good look at himself and how he was relating to his congregation.

"I'm preaching to impress people," he told his wife.

"People are impressed," his wife responded.

"I don't know if that's what I want to be communicating to the people in my church," he said.

"Well, smarty, then why don't you change how you preach and what you are trying to say?"

That's exactly what the First Born preacher did. Once he discovered that his motivation had been to impress others, he changed the way in which he approached his sermons, which changed the effect of his preaching on the community. He had used is knowledge of Birth Order to bring about positive results.

The First Born's Search for Love Through Respect, Admiration, and Approval

First Borns' experience of love as being conditioned on their behavior is a heavy burden. The kind of conditional love the First Born experiences depends on where that First Born happens to be looking for love.

At home with family, First Born adults demand conditional love in the form of respect. First Borns want to know that their children listen to them and that their spouse thinks that what they have to say is important. This is a big issue for them, and if family members complain about this need for respect, First Borns may get angry rather than try to change their behavior. That's a tough way to get love and respect, yet it becomes very important for the First Born. The First Born cannot tolerate disagreement from the spouse

because disagreement signifies a loss of love—all those bad
baby times again. First Borns, then, may pursue various strategies to get their spouse to agree with them, such as getting
angry, arguing for long periods of time, or giving the silent
treatment. The First Born thinks that one of those actions will
surely do the trick, although none of them is very positive or
effective. First Borns think it is intolerable to agree to dis-
agree.

When a First Born is hunting around for respect, he or
she looks much different from a First Born who is looking
for admiration and approval. Respect for this First Born guy
or gal means the children had better be obedient and agreeable. The First Born parent demands instant obedience from
the children, because anything else would show disrespect.
If the troops do not snap to attention in less than two seconds, watch out for a blow-up. Love is lost again.

The kind of respect that First Borns are searching for is
not really compatible with love. Who wants to love a drill
sergeant? Who wants to spend every day worried that he or
she may be considered disrespectful and then have to pay
the price? It's not an easy way to love for the First Born or
for the people he or she calls family.

The kind of respect demanded by a First Born insists that
others look up to them. A healthier way to approach this
would be to seek respect that values the other person.
Because love does not flow uphill, it is tough to love a First
Born who seeks respect by demanding it, rather than earning
it. By seeking respect on their own terms, therefore, First
Borns are actually chasing love away. What they end up with
is obedience that is not heartfelt, no real respect, and the
underpinnings of a rebellion that will explode some day after
family members have been required to do whatever was necessary to keep peace in the house for way too many years.

Well, children should respect their parents. There's no
way around that one. Think about it, though: First Borns who

demand this type of respect from their children may be getting a forced and most likely faked respect without any love.

Parents earn respect by being reasonable, firm, flexible, and responsive, and by listening to their children also get love from them. First Borns who demand unreasoning obedience from their children do not get respect or love. As a result, the search for that elusive four-letter word goes on and on for the First Born.

Love between children and their parents is fostered during those times when children believe that they are on the same level as their parents. They feel this when their parents sit on the floor and play with them, when their parents listen to their ideas, and when they are friends with them as adults.

Children remember those times. One young boy about to enter junior high school wrote a wonderful letter to his father on his father's birthday. He told his father that he considered him to be one of his best friends and that he knew his father was always there for him. The boy did not write about what his father gave him for Christmas or what kind of house they lived in, but about the times they wrestled on the living room floor and about how he loved it when his dad included him in special father-son outings. "Dad, I always knew you loved me because you listened to me and that made me the person I am today," the letter said. "I especially liked it when you let me say what I felt, even if we didn't always agree."

The father was thrilled by what his son had written. Although this father happens to be an Only and the son happens to be a Second, this letter provides a terrific example for a First Born of the value of listening and earning respect. Children are very smart, just like their parents. They know when someone, especially an adult, is being condescending and demanding respect when it is not deserved or warranted. Here is a father who treated his son, not as an equal, but as a whole person who has thoughts and feelings. This father had earned the respect and the love of his son the hard way—but, of course, the father would never in a million years say that anything he had done for his son had been hard.

Away from home, First Borns seek admiration and approval, because they feel that they can't use the power they exert at home to gain the respect they desire. While First Borns seek agreement with others, they do not insist that others agree with them unless they see themselves in a superior position. In that case, they act like they are home again and go back to their demanding ways.

A First Born can be hard to convince when he or she is seeking agreement. Rather than seeking merit in someone else's opinion, a First Born looks for ways to get that person to agree with his or her ideas. Even when First Borns know that the other person is right, they may argue because to do otherwise would be to lose respect, which, in their vision, substitutes for love.

> "There was never yet an uninteresting life. Such a thing is an impossibility. Inside of the dullest interior there is a drama, a comedy, and a tragedy."
>
> —Mark Twain

So there go the First Borns, out the door to try and impress the world. They want to impress so they can win esteem, so they will be noticed, so people will think they are really something. Well, good for them. First Borns like to impress by showing off some of their possessions as well as their own personality traits. They might brag about a great trip they have taken, and if they have a new car, you can bet they will take it for a swing through the neighborhood. They will absolutely be in heaven if they can offer you some "insider" information that will make you think they are pretty cool.

There was a First Born chiropractor who was really confident of his ability to impress others. He knew that all he usually had to do was get people into his office and they

[handwritten marginalia: This too is Christopher. And my sister Mary.]

would be taken by his knowledge and his expertise. One day a potential client called and asked if he could come in for an examination that would prepare him for some alternative therapy. The First Born sprung into action. He wasn't supportive of the alternative therapy, but he felt that if he could just get this patient into the office, he would see what a great doctor he was.

When the client came in the chiropractor gave him an extensive examination, including a blood workup. The client had not asked for the blood work, but the chiropractor was sure he would appreciate it because it was such an impressive thing to do. The results showed various kinds of correctable abnormalities in the blood cells. "Who would not be impressed by that?" thought the First Born.

The patient was not impressed, however, because the examination did not pave the way for the next level of therapy and he had to pay for extensive blood work he had not requested. Like many First Borns would have been, this chiropractor was taken by surprise when he found out that the patient was not impressed by what he thought was highly impressive behavior.

First Borns are like that; well, some of them anyway. The smart ones learn about their behavioral tendencies. Wouldn't it have been great if the chiropractor had first discussed with the patient what he was thinking of doing. Let's hope he did it the next time.

In order to find ways to impress others, First Borns often dream about their future achievements. That's not necessarily a bad thing. How else would we know how far we can reach? Where we could go? First Borns get so caught up in their dreaming ways, however, that they often forget about achieving things in the here and now. Compared to winning the Nobel Peace Prize or being named Citizen of the Year, the everyday business of working seems pretty mundane.

Since they find work less exciting than dreams, First

Borns can appear lazy. They may go about their work with resignation rather than enthusiasm. When a task is done, a First Born tends to feel relief rather than satisfaction, a phenomenon that you have most likely witnessed or experienced yourself. It's a "There, it's done. Are you happy now?" feeling instead of a "Wow, I did it and I feel great!" reaction.

What happens is that the more a First Born dreams, the more he or she decreases his or her chance of actually reaching the dream. It's okay to dream part of the time, but if you dream all of the time you can't get very far.

One positive way for First Borns to get around this type of behavior is to use a "Done List" for recording all of the accomplishments of a day and thereby generate some feelings of satisfaction within themselves. The Done List would also provide relief from the feelings of guilt over those things left undone, in that it would illustrate that there simply was not enough time to do everything.

As part of their general quest for love, First Borns actively seek approval from their superiors, sometimes going to great lengths. They may work overtime without pay, do work at the boss's house for free, or do special favors for their employer so they will get noticed. We all have a name for this kind of man or woman at work. You can use your own right here, but doesn't it help to understand why they do it? It should.

Because approval is so important to them, First Borns tend to feel extremely guilty about any negative feedback they receive. They will castigate themselves unmercifully for behaving in such a way as to merit a reprimand. Then they will work hard to let those above them know that they are trying hard to correct whatever problems were pointed out. These First Borns really go overboard.

To conserve love, First Borns tend to be compromisers. When friends want something from them, First Borns will definitely deliver. They will do whatever is necessary, even if it means a hardship for them or their family. First Borns

unfair,
unfair,
unfair!
— this is
Christoph

actually tend to put others' needs before those of their own
family, all the while expecting the family to agree with them
that this is the right or necessary thing to do. Family members
think that this attitude is terribly unfair and the relationship
between the First Born and the family will suffer as a result.

Because First Borns feel like there is no love for them in
the world, they believe that they cannot ask for what they
want. Their controlling thought is that no one would want to
give them anything, anyway, because no one cares about
them. So rather than taking the risk of asking, they try to
seduce others into giving them what they want.

First Borns find hinting around safer than asking, because
they have the option of backing off if it becomes apparent
that they are not going to get what they want. First Borns are
great hinters. The hinting may be so subtle that the other
person may not realize they are doing it. For example, a First
Born employee may want to get on the day shift, but instead
of just asking his supervisor about it, he will say something
like, "My wife would love it if I were working the day shift,"
or "I've been on nights for three years now," or "Joe got on
days and he hasn't been here as long as I have."

A First Born might also focus on what the employer
wants. For example, he might ask his employer if it would
be better for the employer if the First Born were to go on
the day shift. If the employer says no, the First Born cannot
say, "I want to go on days, anyway."

Without having confidence in being loved, a First Born
has a terrible time being forthright, stating what she wants or
feels. Because of that, when you ask a First Born what she
thinks the answer is usually, "I don't know. What do you
think?" Does that answer drive you crazy? Then you are
probably not a First Born.

Once you tell a First Born what you think, she will tell you
what she thinks, unless it differs from what you think. In that
case the First Born will either try to agree with you or will

fudge her answer so as not to contradict what you have said. She does not want to lose whatever love you might extend.

One First Born woman had been married a number of years but still found it hard to say what she felt, wanted, or needed. As a result, he never really knew how she felt about him. This poor guy had to guess at what she wanted, and as an Only he was unable to do that.

Eventually, after their children were grown, they separated, even though they had great love for each other. The relationship broke up largely because, as a First Born, the wife had been unable to communicate her thoughts to the husband. Of course, she wasn't the only one to blame. His inability to understand her also contributed to the failure of the marriage. If this couple had known about Birth Order Personality, there is a good chance that they might have been able to continue their relationship and to enjoy it as well.

The old image of a First Born being a great leader is totally altered with Birth Order Personality. It might make sense that First Borns with younger siblings would be good leaders at home, and that those leadership skills would carry over into other areas of the First Born's life. Actually, the opposite is true. First Borns tend to be overlooked when promotions are being handed out.

First Borns get confused and angry when this happens— after all they have done extra work for the boss, come in early, and done what they consider to be better work then anyone else. As a result, they end up feeling even more unloved and as if all their efforts have been for nothing.

Things don't have to stay this way for the First Born. There is a world of opportunity and hope out there and more than enough love to go around—honest.

. The First Born will be glad to know that there is a Second Born just waiting to take on their own emotional hot potato. Second Borns are you ready? It's your turn to take a good look in the mirror.

● ● ● ● ●

> Ask not what your country can do for you,
> ask what you can do for your country.
> —John F. Kennedy (Second Born)

Chapter Seven

That Won't Work;
It's Not Good Enough:
The Second Born

Stay calm, Second Borns. We can get you through this, and you will still have time left over so you can go get more work done and solve the problems of the world.

Here's a Birth Order filled with writers, artists, teachers, editors, financial wizards, decorators, and finish carpenters. Any job that requires a mind and heart for details will most likely be filled by a Second Born. Perfection is the key word here. Second Borns love to keep themselves and their "things" in very particular order.

All those friends who make you take off your shoes in their house, who never seem to be listening when you give them what you think is some pretty solid advice, and who always pick the lint off your sweatshirt surely act like Second Borns.

— I do that

One female client who saw Cliff Isaacson on a regular basis would always spend a few minutes straightening out his desk before they began a session. She would push the pencils to one side, stack up his books, and move his papers into some kind of orderly grouping. The woman was convinced that Isaacson messed up his desk on purpose, just to drive her nuts. Now, there's a Second Born who knows a disaster when she sees one.

Here's a quick test for all you Second Borns who can't quite decide if this is the chapter for you. Get out your pencil, which no doubt will be sharpened and sitting right next to your clean notepad, and get ready to make a few check marks. Be honest. When you think about yourself, realize that nothing in this book is written to be critical. This is simply a new way to see yourself, and it will help you to understand why you act, react, and live the way you do. Besides that, isn't it a heck of a lot of fun to find out all these things? Ready? Here we go.

Remember that you are psychologically a Second Born if five or more of the following are true for you. Have fun, and don't be afraid to go ahead and smile.

Second Born Birth Order Personality Characteristics

- You feel like others can do things better than you can.
- You feel like others do not care about how you feel.
- You pay attention to details.
- You are a perfectionist in some areas but not others.
- You suppress feelings.
- You dislike gossip.
- You like accounting but not math.

I do like math – but not tax accounting!

- You are artistic.
- You look for flaws.
- You find it hard to give praise.
- You are chronologically second, sixth, tenth, or four-teenth in the family.

There. Wasn't that kind of fun? Welcome to the wonderful, creative, challenging, and never dull world of the Second Born. As you have probably already noticed by reading the Birth Order Matrix in Chapter 3, the Second Born has more than a wealth of the good, the really good, and the even better than that. Flipping back to that chapter as you read these pages will help you keep things in perspective.

Those charts will give you a bird's-eye view of the Second Born Personality. This peacemaking Birth Order starts developing these traits at a young age, and once you know the details about the Second Born, you may find yourself slapping your hand against your forehead and say, "Wow, was my brother ever a Second Born!"

Well, if this brother was always trying to set up family agreements and did whatever he could to get everyone to get along, then we are talking Second Born. Every family has one—and needs one. The Second Borns are sensitive to anger, have a neglected inner child, use tons of logic and love to evaluate.

Before we trace the psychological history of a Second Born, consider these few key traits that separate the Second Born from the rest of the world. These commonly held feelings, emotions, actions, and thoughts of the Second Born may manifest themselves in a variety of ways. Remember that not every Second Born will have all of these characteristics. We remain individuals, no matter what Birth Order Personality we slip into each morning.

Second Born Personality Traits

- Displays perfectionism
- Uses logic
- Does lots of evaluating
- Acts as a peacemaker — *when allowed*
- Is sensitive to anger
- Follows rules
- Is a strict parent — *was*
- Is very self-disciplined
- Is honest
- Is determined
- Is a helpful friend
- Loves to keep the house and office neat — *too much work*
- Finishes projects
- Experiences intense emotions
- Often corrects others — *tries not to, but it's hard*
- Is most likely to give up smoking or drinking, or to stay on a tough exercise routine

This is by no means a complete list of Second Born Birth Order Personality traits, but it is a place to get acclimated before we head off into the tundra. Considering this list of traits may help you to stand back and take a long, hard look at yourself and at other Second Borns as well.

A Second Born mother in a Midwestern city learned from Cliff Isaacson that her chronological first-born son was a psychological Second Born. Not only was this boy exactly like his mother, he was that way partially because of her. Once this woman understood that her first-born son was really a Second Born, she decided to treat him differently. For years she had been guided by the ideas that many of us have embraced about chronological birth order.

This woman's son had always been a strong leader, but his almost compulsive behavior had always mystified her. Her son would notice if she moved the Chapstick on his night-stand, for example, or if she put one of the books he had alphabetized in the wrong section of the bookshelf.

"I had always looked at him as having a first-born per-sonality and never compared him to myself, because, well, because he was a first-born," she told Isaacson. "We've always had a wonderful relationship, but once I understood that he was a Second Born, and that he was so similar to me, our relationship got even better, and I was able to play on his sense of humor and under-stand him even better."

One of the first things this mother did was to tell her son not to make his bed in the morning. "What?" he said, astounded at the very idea. "You mean just leave it like this, all torn up with the covers hanging out?"

"Yes, sweetie," she told him, throwing his pillow on the floor.

"Mom," he said, trying not to cry, "this will drive me crazy."

"Listen," she said, pulling him toward her in an embrace, "you need to see that the world won't fall apart and that life will go on if your bed isn't made everyday."

> "Discourage litigation. Persuade your neighbors to compromise when-ever you can. Point out to them how the nominal winner is often a real loser—in fees, expenses, and waste of time. As a peacemaker the lawyer has a superior opportu-nity of being a good man. There will still be business enough."
>
> —Abraham Lincoln (Second Born)

—I agree!

This was a kid who tucked in the corners of his sheets and lined up all his shoes and did all his homework a month early. He also had his own sense of humor. He had prob-ably figured out he was a Second Born before his mother had ever talked to Cliff Isaacson.

"What about you, Mom?"

"What about me?"

"You go take your bed apart."

"Are you kidding?" she laughed back. "All those germs from the air will get in there."

Who said you can't have fun with Birth Order? This mother used her new knowledge to understand the intimate workings of her son's mind and to get him to look at himself in a new way. After she had asked him leave his bed unmade a few times, she noticed that it was no longer such a big deal for him—although, to this day, he still manages to keep the bed looking fairly perfect about 360 days a year.

Second Borns have the taste of competition in their mouths from day one. The First Born gives the Second Born a hard time as often as possible. Step into a family situation where there is a First and Second Born and you will notice immediately that the First Born loves to talk for the Second Born. If you ask a Second Born "What's your name?" the First Born will reply before the Second Born can get her mouth open, "Her name is Rachel and she is in third grade and she likes dolls."

The First Born will constantly give the Second Born a run for her money. If the Second Born is trying to show something new to Grandpa or Grandma, you can bet the farm that within a few minutes the First Born will come up with something bigger and better to get all the attention. The competition can easily make the Second Born feel inadequate and more than a little hateful toward the overbearing First Born. A Second Born does not feel a loss of the parents' love to the First Born, but rather a sense of competition from the First Born sibling. Competition is extremely hard to counter.

The competition from the First Born makes the Second Born feel inadequate because it seems as if nothing he or she does is good enough. Whatever Second Borns can do, the older sibling can do better—or at least has done already.

"She's still a pest"

Who hasn't heard this one? "I'm bigger than you are," or "I've already been to first grade," or "I got that for my birthday last year." Oh, the poor Second Born is in for it.

With a take-charge First Born elbowing his or her way into every scene of a Second Born's life, that Second Born will continue to feel inadequate, because the older brother or sister has been there and done that. If the Second Born gets a B in class, the First Born will show up with an A. When Second Born makes the soccer team, First Born will make the select soccer team. When Second Born announces his or her first crush, the First Born will talk about his or her last three.

It doesn't matter that the First Born may be more capable simply because of the age difference. The Second Born will only know that he or she is inadequate compared to that First Born. Many Second Borns will automatically say things like, "I can't do anything right," or "It doesn't matter what I do; it's never going to be good enough." Some Second Borns struggle their entire lives with feelings of inadequacy created by an early decision to say that it won't matter how hard they try or what they do. Others can overcome their early experiences and move on with the knowledge that anything is possible.

How the Second Born Copes with Feelings of Inadequacy

Many Second Borns learn from these early experiences that it's impossible to do everything perfectly. In their little minds they are thinking, "Well, okay, I can't do that because they do that, but I can do this and make this mine, and I can be better at it than anyone in the whole world." Thus, the Second Born becomes a perfectionist, but only in a few areas.

Professionally, the adult Second Born will try to get every detail right. Second Borns tend to gravitate toward jobs that require detail, because it gives them a chance to be perfect, and that's something they are constantly striving toward.

Many Second Born children, including Isaacson's own Second Born, will go crazy if they are working on a drawing or a piece of school work and they make a mistake. Sometimes, erasing it isn't quite good enough. Many Second Born children will throw away page after page until they can complete the work without using an eraser or making a wrong move.

Interestingly enough, Second Borns don't carry their perfectionism into every area of their lives. The top of the bureau might be clean, but their underwear drawer might be a disaster area. A Second Born boy's room could be a mess, for example, but you can bet that when he heads off to basketball practice, his sneakers will be spotless and everything will be lined up and tidy in his gym bag.

Sometimes Second Borns may perform perfectly but still may not be able to overcome their feelings of inadequacy, thanks again to that overbearing First Born. The desire to be perfect can be so strong in Second Borns that their fantasies about performing as the greatest in something can actually take the place of the real performance. To a Second Born, doing something in one's mind is much better than doing it not so perfectly for real.

It's no surprise then that Second Borns have a bit of a hard time giving someone a pat on the back. Inside their interesting minds, they feel as if someone has made them feel inadequate so they are going to return the favor and make others feel just the same way. The reason Second Borns do not compliment others is that they believe that compliments hurt them as children because First Borns got them all the time. They feel they will hurt someone else if they themselves give out a compliment.

Instead of telling someone, "Wow, that was just tremendous. You did a super job," the Second Born is more likely to say something like, "Well, if you had done x, y, or z, it would have been so much better. Do you think Second Borns need to take a deep breath and relax once in a while? Sometimes they can be a bit more subtle when they try to compliment, but none of this from-the-heart talk will come from Second Borns until they feel good about themselves.

The testy little Second Born can't quite seem to forget what happened during those early years when the word *compassion* seemed to be absent from that First Born's lips. Second Born children believe that First Borns have no compassion for them and will do whatever it takes to get the attention or whatever else they need—that if they can take from a Second Born they will, and that the First Borns don't care about a Second Born's feelings. If a parent or other adult gives in to the demands of the First Born, and ends up ignoring the Second Born, the Second Born will also feel as if the adult doesn't really care about his or her feelings.

Feelings then, for the Second Born, are shifted from the front of the mind and heart to the back. Rather than continue to feel bad because of that goofy First Born, they try not to feel at all. Combine all those feelings of inadequacy with the perception that emotions should be avoided at all costs, and you have the supporting foundation for the Second Born Birth Order Personality.

It makes sense that a Second Born would throw feelings out the window and embrace logic. Consider the Second Born husband who listens to his wife describe why she is unhappy. He may look as if he cares about what she is saying, and his eyes might even go soft, but then he blows it by mentioning all of the logical reasons why his wife should be happy. "We have a nice house, there's beer in the fridge, the car starts; how could you not be happy?"

There's a Second Born who sits on his emotions. This guy probably made his wife feel worse than she already did. She probably would've loved it if he had just taken here her in his arms and said something simple like, "I know sweetie; sometimes life is tough." This guy, however, would rather hand out advice or analyze his wife's feelings. All that logic makes him feel more adequate, and isn't that what he wants anyway?

A Second Born's propensity to point out flaws and little things that just aren't quite as perfect as they should be is not meant to hurt the person on the receiving end. In a Second Born's mind, the quest for perfection extends to everyone. In making critical comments and keeping praise to a minimum, the Second Borns are only trying to help someone else reach the same level of perfection that they are seeking.

All this criticism is more than tough to handle if you happen to be in a relationship with a Second Born, however. One Second Born man was just a bit puzzled when his wife left him after he had worked very hard to be the "perfect" husband, did all the chores around the house, never once thought about other women, and was always around when his wife needed him. Imagine the shocked look on his face when his wife told him she was leaving. She told him she had just had it with his criticisms, and that although he was great in many areas, she simply wanted to be with a man who would listen to her and care about her feelings. Friends and family members of this couple were just as astounded as the husband was. "How could she leave him?" they all asked. "He's perfect."

"Perfect" is one thing, but this Second Born had come off as unfeeling and insensitive to the needs of his wife. She never returned after leaving him, because she felt that no matter what happened, he would always put her feelings toward the bottom of his list of things that were important. That is, if "feelings" were on his list at all.

Although Second Borns are critical of others, it must be noted that they themselves don't care much about having praise thrown their way. In their quest for perfection, they would much rather be told what they did wrong than what they did right. Yet criticism aimed toward Second Borns that is filled with irritation, anger, or disappointment will drive them wild. They are only interested in learning what they did wrong so that they can do it better.

> "My eye is educated to discover anything on the ground, as chestnuts, etc. It is probably wholesomer to look at the ground much than at the heavens."
>
> —Henry David Thoreau (Second Born)

Forget about sending a note to the Second Born down the hall telling him he did a terrific job on the proposal. He'll want to know what he could have done better. The same holds true for children. That sixth-grade paper might be a winner to you, but the Second Born is always looking for ways to make the sentences stronger or push the research one step further—as well as reasons to throw the whole thing out the window and start over.

Parents might be dismayed at their Second Born teenaged daughter, whose need for perfection is expressed in her preoccupation with her appearance. She tries on different makeup, combs her hair in different styles, tries out various facial expressions, practices her smile, and puts expression into her eye movements. One girl confessed that she watched herself in the mirror while talking on the telephone so she could study her own appearance.

Second Borns (both girls and boys) who devote a lot of attention to their appearance can be quite attractive. You can see the perfectionism in their walk, clothing, body language, and facial expressions.

Additional Second Born Attitudes and Behaviors

If the man who steered the Titanic across the ocean and directly into an iceberg, had known about Second Borns he may have never left the dock. Captain Edward John Smith offered the world some interesting insights into the behavior of Second Borns. At least one would-be passenger, who just happened to have been Cliff Isaacson's grandfather, ended up being thankful for this Second Born behavior.

Smart man that he was, Grandpa was in the pub having a great time on the day that the Titanic was scheduled to sail when he realized he had better get on down to the boat dock as soon as possible. Well, Captain Smith, in typical Second Born fashion, had very strict rules about people boarding his ship. If you were late, tough luck—or good luck as it turned out for the Isaacson family. Grandpa was not allowed to board the boat because he was late, so he went back to the pub—and spent the rest of his life celebrating his good fortune.

We all know what happened to the Titanic. Smith had listened so intently so the so-called experts who had said that the ship could never sink that he took risks in the interest of speed on their way to New York, disregarding his own crew's warnings about the danger of the icebergs. Smith was chosen for his job because he had twenty-five years of experience and had proven himself to be a highly skilled captain. Second Borns do a good job, gain respect, and generate confidence. But, they are also governed by a feeling of inadequacy when they are given a lot of responsibility. At that point, they listen to experts rather than trust their own judgment. Second Borns, who fight against what they know and, instead, blindly accept what the experts tell them they are supposed to know, will find it to be tough going.

In the professional world, perfection-seeking Second

Borns will often be found in front offices, where they can try to orchestrate the world into some kind of perfect balance. Second Borns make wonderful receptionists, administrative assistants, and office managers. Using their professional, businesslike, and logical minds and personalities, Second Borns thrive on jobs where they can organize and handle many details.

Their perfectionism can also lead Second Borns into accounting professions. Throwing all those numbers into the air, watching them land, and then sorting them out is an exciting challenge for the Second Born. Ask your accountant and banker about their Birth Order; ten to one they are Second Borns.

Many artists who strive for technical perfection in painting, drawing, architecture, music, and some writing fields are also Second Borns.

This drive for perfection in the professional world can be a plus or minus, depending on how you look at it. Second Borns tend to work on details rather than pursue goals. Usually, they rise to a certain level in their profession and either stay there or switch careers. A Second Born would rather try to achieve perfection where they are than risk being unsuccessful at a higher level. That's exactly why many Second Borns from small towns tend to stay there rather than heading to the big city. They would rather be that big fish in a small pond.

One interesting result of all these Second Borns staying put is that in rural America—which is, after all, a pretty hefty chunk of the world—Second Borns are in charge. They are school board members and presidents, mayors, and heads of hospital boards, and they can whip up a community for a good cause faster than you can say, "You made a mistake."

It's also interesting to see what Second Borns do once they take over. On a town board or city council, for example, they would much rather work on road improvements than on designing a new master plan for the community.

And how about those rules? Second Borns love to follow the rules. Consider the following example. A kindergartner came home from school one day complaining to his mother that his teacher had said he wasn't ready to be in her class. The boy's mother was astounded. "What do you mean?" she asked him, knowing that her son was very bright. "She said I have to go to preschool first," he told her.

Mom did a little background research and found out that the teacher had an unwritten rule that every child in her class should have attended a preschool. It didn't matter to her how bright the child was or if the child had stayed home with a parent who was a teacher; she believed that all kids should attend preschool. This teacher was a true Second Born.

This Second Born teacher also had a natural inclination to give any First Born a hard time—even if the First Born was one of her students. This boy was a First Born, and it didn't help the situation that the boy's mother seemed overprotective of her son. The teacher gave the little boy a hard time no matter what he did, especially since he was breaking her preschool rule. Once she reprimanded him on the playground for refusing to play with a group of boys, "Mom," he said when he got home that afternoon, "those boys were throwing rocks and it would've been wrong to play with them."

After the boy's mother had told the school principal how the teacher was treating her son, the principal had a little chat with the Second Born teacher. She, in turn, tried to make the principal understand her set of rules. Second Borns govern themselves by rules, and they want everyone else to follow the rules, also.

When the teacher had her back up against the wall, her instinct was probably to use her own authority to extricate herself from the situation. Second Borns like authority and they tend to deal with conflict by establishing their own authority. They often tend to appeal to authority figures or try to establish policies that will give them rules by which to operate if none are already in place.

Let's address some of the other Second Born traits and characteristics. A Second Born's sense of determination and self-discipline pays off when it comes to doing something like losing weight, ending a smoking habit, or saving money. If a Second Born makes up his or her mind to run a marathon, win a Pulitzer, or fly to the moon, it will probably happen.

Second Borns also dislike deadlines, and to avoid a deadline, they will either complete the task way ahead of time or they may procrastinate until the last second. Second Born college students, for example, will either write a paper a month before they have to hand it in, or they will pull an all-nighter and put the last period on the paper two minutes before class starts.

Let's not forget the great peacemaking side of the Second Born Personality. Because Second Borns hate anger, they tend to use their logic to solve conflict. Let's give Second Borns a little credit for this positive aspect of their personality. They might not make you love them by telling you exactly why and how you screwed up to cause this conflict in the first place, but they do get the job done—and who in their right mind couldn't use a little more peace?

As we mentioned earlier, Second Borns often have an artistic side, and they can feel strongly about the way they choose to express themselves. Popular singer Britney Spears is one Second Born whose artistic side of her Birth Order Personality is out there for the world to see. Britney was criticized recently for taking on a sexier look, and she could not believe the fuss. This classic Second Born saw herself as an artist, and considered her style of dress to be a way of expressing herself artistically, not of advertising her sexuality.

Our Second Born Personality, like all Personalities, is a complex, interesting bundle of humanness that, in this case, has the willpower to move mountains.

While this Birth Order Personality is busy perfecting one corner of the world after another, the unsuspecting Third Born is waiting to make an appearance, not daring to open his eyes until the last second. When those eyes are opened, guess what he sees? A big, old Second Born eager as anything to pass off a truckload of feelings of inadequacy to the next kid in line.

Second Borns, rejoice; it's time to pass the Birth Order Personality book over to your little brother or sister. Here you go, Third Borns. It's been a wait, but it's finally your turn.

Fear is the little darkroom where
negatives are developed.
—Michael Pritchard

Chapter Eight

No Problem;
It Doesn't Bother Me Any:
The Third Born

Hello, Third Borns, and come on down. No sense standing around, waiting for something that you might be afraid of that doesn't even exist. No matter what your big brothers and sisters told you, being a Third Born is not really that bad. It's probably not a good idea now to tell you to pay attention, because you have been doing that your entire life, but it would really help if you want to learn more about this great Birth Order Personality.

This is a Birth Order that is full of interesting twists and turns. The men and women who call this Personality home can soar if they know what has motivated them to do, think, and then act in specific ways.

And no, you are not just the runt of the family. It isn't true that you won't and can't amount to anything just because all your big brothers and sisters have done or acquired every-thing first. The world can be yours if you can study yourself and discover how your Birth Order Personality has equipped you to do so.

For starters, how about taking a look at Third Born Birth Order characteristics? If you have been shifting from foot to foot as you read through the previous pages and haven't yet recognized yourself, this could be the Birth Order you have been waiting for.

Remember, if you can see yourself in at least five of these examples, then this is it for you, kid. You are a Third Born Birth Order Personality. Go find your best friend to go through the following with you, and be honest.

Third Born Birth Order Personality Characteristics

- You do not like being scared.
- You feel for the underdog.
- You get lots of ideas.
- You are friendly to many but have only one or two close friends.
- You like to help others.
- You are pleased when others are pleased.
- You make comparisons in your mind.
- You have to be emotionally strong so nothing bothers you.
- You cannot stand up for yourself unless you are angry.
- You hate being bored so you keep busy.
- You like interruptions if they are interesting.
- You can change direction at a moment's notice.
- You are often late because you do not like to get to places early.

- You are offended when others do not listen to your ideas.
- You try not to let anything bother you.

Let's get right into this and find out what makes the Third Born Birth Order Personalities of the world tick. It will be an adventure—one that will surely keep all the Third Borns from being bored.

Third Borns really do learn how to be afraid of fear. The Third Born sees fear as an enemy to be overcome before it overcomes him or her. Where did this come from? Just look back a few pages. That delightful Second Born spent lots of hours trying to pass on feelings of inadequacy to the Third Born sibling.

Who wants to feel inadequate? None of the Birth Order Personalities would find this particularly entrancing. The discomfort of inadequacy prompts the Second Born to give this feeling to the Third Born. Talk about the hot potato. "Here," says the Second Born, "you can have all this junk because I sure don't want it." Thus stands the Third Born with piles of stuff he or she does not want.

Second Borns, bless their little hearts, do a terrific job of finding ways to make the Third Born feel bad. Anything a Third Born does, thinks, or says is up for grabs as far as the Second Born is concerned. It is easy for Second Borns to make the Third Born feel insecure because they are older, more mature, far wiser in the ways of the world, more capable, and more aggressive than the Third Born.

How many of us have been on the giving or receiving end of some of this? How about the Second Born who gets the Third Born to take over the chores? Then there's the pressure the Third Born puts at him- or herself to try and think up something the Second Born has not already tried or succeeded at.

One Second Born brother was paying his sister a dime or quarter to do chores that he was getting paid fifty cents and a dollar to do. This little guy thought he had a great gig going until his mother caught on. Once, when he took on the job of shoveling an elderly neighbor's driveway, he talked his sister into doing it for a dollar when the neighbor was going to pay him five dollars.

"Well," he answered, when his mother asked him what kind of racket he was running, "she was dumb enough to do it so I thought, 'What the heck.'"

When his sister found out what he had been doing, she told him, "You make me sick."

Way to go, Third Born. Now that you are onto the Second Born's behavior, maybe life will finally get a little easier.

This doesn't mean that the Third Born necessarily feels inadequate every time he or she falls into a trap set by a Second Born brother or sister. Rather than feeling inadequate, the Third Born actually feels vulnerable to the Second Born's attacks. Eventually, the Third Born comes to feel vulnerable to virtually everyone. Consequently, from early on, Third Borns live in a world in which they feel that anyone can get to them any time they wish.

You Third Borns might be saying, "Wow, that explains everything." It's a good start. But there is more. Want some more details before we plunge ahead? Here are some traits that will help you get an even better feeling for who you are.

Third Born Birth Order Personality Traits

- Feels vulnerable
- Has emotional strength
- Is rescuing and helpful
- Uses humor as emotional defense
- Has a tendency to think comparatively

- Often uses the phrase, "No problem"
- Has a putdown sense of humor
- Is a pleaser
- Is creative
- Finds it hard to work with others
- Is friendly but has only one or two close friends
- Often experiences boredom
- Is a bottom line thinker, leaves out details
- May experience anxiety/panic
- Believes in Robin Hood–type justice

There are plenty of reasons for the Third Born Birth Order Personality to be happy. The Third Born does not develop a system of perfectionism like the Second Born. Instead, the Third Born must figure out how to get along in a world in which others appear threatening. No easy chore, especially in a world where those Second Borns are constantly driving you crazy.

How the Third Born Copes with Feelings of Vulnerability

The Third Born eventually goes to Mom for some answers about how to deal with the constant and various forms of harassment being inflicted by the Second Born. It has not been a pretty picture. We've all heard this type of bickering— in fact, some of it may be going on right now in the room next to which you are sitting. Little fights, bigger fights, really big fights. Small "you can't do anything" putdowns, probably a little name-calling. Anything goes when the busy Second Born is trying to get to the Third Born.

The mother eventually gets exasperated (and who in the world wouldn't?) at her inability to make things better. Here comes the good part: Mother finally tells the Third Born that if he or she just ignores the Second Born, the Second Born will lose interest and won't do it anymore.

Third Borns are so cool they believe their mothers, which is what we are supposed to do. They can't believe it when ignoring the taunts the Second Borns throws their way actually works. It works like magic and leaves the Second Borns with no clue as to what to do next.

For the Third Borns this is like an early Christmas present or having ice cream for breakfast. It's a terrific new discovery. Now Third Borns have a way of dealing with a threatening world—by not letting it bother them. This kind of a "don't worry, be happy" attitude can change a Third Born's life.

Consider the following example. A grandfather sat in the living room with his feet up on his favorite recliner and watched as his Third Born grandson interacted with his two older sisters—which, he though, was surely more entertaining than anything on television. The Third Born had been a good Birth Order Personality student, whether or not he actually knew it.

The sisters were relentless. They tried every trick in the book to get a rise out of him.

"You have the weirdest hair," said one sister.

"I know; isn't it something," said the Third Born.

"No one is ever going to go out on a date with you," said the other precious sister.

"Maybe not," said the boy.

"I'm smarter in math than you are," tried the first sister again.

"That's nice," said our mighty Third Born.

"Well, I'm going to a sleepover and you aren't," said the second sister.

"That's nice," said the Third Born.

On it went for forty-five minutes with the Third Born saying, "That's nice," about 123 times. Finally, the girls gave up and left and the Third Born, feeling quite adequate, thank you very much, finally had some peace.

Those of us who are not Third Borns can hardly believe that a person is able to act like the little Third Born boy. These Third Borns look amazing to those of us who, as children, dealt with putdowns by shouting back, throwing a harsher putdown in someone's face, asking for help, or simply leaving the room to find another place to play. Third Borns just do not let it bother them, and whoever tries to get to them eventually gets tired and leaves the area.

Psychologically, it is difficult to act as if taunts do not bother you and even more difficult to actually not let them bother you. The Third Born is able to accomplish this feat by making an effort to turn off his or her fear. The Third Born knows that fear makes him or her vulnerable to others—that fear cannot be tolerated and has to go.

> "I must create a system or be enslaved by another man's. I will not reason and compare. My business is to create."
>
> —William Blake

Amazingly, Third Borns are capable of dealing with this pressure beginning at a young age. One ten-year-old Third Born, for example, came home from school and started sorting through her day for her mother. She casually mentioned the fact that she was one of only two girls in the entire class not invited to a birthday party.

The mother was aghast. She immediately felt sorry for her daughter and couldn't believe that a mother would allow her child to pass out invitations at school and then talk about the party with the entire class.

"Oh, honey, I'm sorry about the party," said the mother.

"Mom, it's not that big of a deal."

"Is that what you think?"

"Well, I felt a little bad about it but, Mom, if she doesn't know how much fun I am, it's her loss."

"Are you kidding?"

"Nope."

"That's really something, honey. I'm proud of you."

"Mom, stuff like that happens to me all the time. You just have to deal with it or it will ruin your whole day."

How's that for a great attitude? Not being invited to the party was a subtle type of putdown, but this little girl knew just what to do. Of course, she had plenty of practice from living with a Second Born brother.

One thing that does happen to Third Borns as they try to overcome fear is that they actually develop a fear of fear itself. This emotion feeds on itself, and the Third Born boy or girl may experience problems that arise from an exploding secondary fear that others do not experience. Secondary fear can lead to panic attacks, anxiety attacks, various phobias—especially agoraphobia, a morbid fear of wide-open spaces—and excessive worry. In adults, it can lead to overprotecting children, constantly attacking others to keep them from appearing threatening, and searching for ways to conquer fear.

One particular Third Born who did not know how to deal with her fear would stuff it inside of herself and ended up in the hospital several times, not even remembering how she'd gotten there. She had suffered psychotic episodes as a result of being overwhelmed with fear. Some Third Borns actually faint from fear-induced anxiety without knowing that they are afraid.

Third Borns who do conquer fear become absolutely fearless. Since fear lurks in the background of their emotions, however, fearless Third Borns must constantly prove their fearlessness to themselves and others. They love to take risks and be dared. Bungee jumping? No problem. Skydiving? Get the plane ready. Going first? Here comes the Third Born.

Every new scary challenge requires Third Borns to demonstrate their absolute courage yet again. They must constantly act as if they have no fear. Third Born children often get hurt or into trouble in the process of trying to prove to others that they are fearless by taking dares.

Overcoming fear is not an easy thing to do, no matter what Birth Order Personality sign we happen to be standing under. The Third Born handles this problem by trying hard to be emotionally strong on the inside. They reason that if they are strong enough, nothing can get to them. This can be accomplished by replacing fear with anger. Anger is such a powerful emotion it wipes out fear. The Third Born may turn on the anger only when fear arises or they may be angry most of the time in order to preclude the possibility of feeling fear. This anger is sometimes directed at others who do not deserve it.

A great example of this kind of Third Born Birth Order Personality behavior was displayed by a woman who had ordered some prints for her wall. When she came to pick them up, she spent a great deal of time looking them over to make certain they were perfect and didn't have any flaws. When she found that a little section of one of the prints did not look quite right, she flew into a rage at the clerk who was handling the transaction.

The flaw in the picture was so tiny you would need a magnifying glass to see it, but to the Third Born it appeared to be a huge defect. In this case, her anger had allowed her to stop feeling afraid—otherwise her fear would have been overwhelming.

This woman sounds like a Second Born with her attention to detail. The important difference is that Second Borns can accept items with flaws if they are the best they can get. They feel good about having seen the flaw and do not become angry over the flaw. This Third Born became angry over the flaw because she saw it as something done deliberately to cheat her. It was the sense of vulnerability that made her look for the flaw in the first place.

Third Borns commonly use the phrase "No problem" when asked to do something or when being thanked for what they have done to signal their strength to others. Other Birth

Order Personalities use this phrase once in a while, but Third Borns use it all the time. Can you do this paper over? No problem. Would you mind driving a hundred miles to drop off this box for me? No problem. Do you realize that you are driving me crazy? No problem.

Fearless Third Born adults are heroes on the battlefield, in emergency rooms and ambulances, and on police forces. They may choose to work as construction workers because they aren't fazed by heights and don't worry about falling. If there is a hazardous task to be completed, or a line of work that could be extremely dangerous, call on the Third Born.

Recently a Third Born found himself in a situation in which he witnessed a man with a gun take a woman hostage. This Third Born openly challenged the hostage taker and was shot and killed. In effect, the Third Born's fearlessness killed him.

Third Borns who cannot conquer their fears may head in the opposite direction of the man who challenged the hostage taker. In fact, ordinary fears may feed a Third Born's anxiety to the point where the Third Born begins hiding at home and totally changes his or her lifestyle. Third Borns may begin to fear going out in public because of what they perceive as a possibility of catching a deadly disease. They may begin to cover their mouths in public, refuse to touch anyone, and shun public events. This might also refuse to speak to groups, ride in airplanes, or call anyone on the telephone. Their world can quickly become limited by their overblown fears.

> "I've developed a new philosophy—I only dread one day at a time."
>
> —Charlie Brown

Third Borns can create anxiety in others without being aware of it themselves. One day a Third Born mother brought her eight-year-old son to see a dentist. The boy was only a little hesitant to come into the office until she told him,

"Don't be afraid." At that point he became terrified to come in. She had created the fear in him by trying to keep him from being afraid.

Third Borns can also create fear in others by going into the attack mode. They feel vulnerable because they do not have an effective defense mode and take the offensive—after all, a good offense is a good defense. With little or no provocation they can verbally (and sometimes physically) attack the other person. For example, a Third Born woman frequently, without any warning, would scold her children and her husband. Her family was at a loss to appease her. It was her sense of vulnerability that drove her to berate friends, acquaintances, store clerks, and even her pastor.

Fortunately, this example is a rarity, but it does illustrate a Third Born's approach to solving the problem of vulnerability. The Third Born has to figure out a way to feel safe in an unsafe world. That is a primary task for him or her.

Third Borns' feelings of vulnerability often keep them from doing what they want to do. The Second Born had always laughed at them, ridiculed them, or taunted them when they had announced what they planned on doing. They learned to go about their business without discussing it. That might be okay for the Third Born, but it's tough for the men and women who deal with them all the time. Guessing games are fun, but not twenty-four hours a day.

Additional Third Born Attitudes and Behaviors

Because they are always dealing with feelings of vulnerability, Third Borns try to keep a distance between themselves and other people in various ways. For example, they may use ideas as a buffer so that people pay attention to the ideas rather than to the Third Born. When a relationship becomes too intimate for them, they may use humor to establish the right distance.

Many Third Borns cannot bring themselves to enter into a permanent relationship. They will use excuses or do what they can to keep from making a commitment that will put them in a vulnerable position.

One fearful Third Born man backed off from his marriage just two weeks before the wedding date, even though he really wanted to get married and was totally in love with his fiancée, whom he lived with. One day this Third Born left for work telling his bride-to-be that he loved her very much. Not more then ten hours later he came home, sat down, and told her that he wanted out of the relationship.

The woman was stunned. She did not know what to say. Here was a man that she loved, was already sharing her life with, and had promised to love forever. She did not know what to do or what was going on.

The man moved out immediately and went back to live with his parents. He didn't even want to talk to the woman he had been planning to marry. In one horrible day, his anxious vulnerability overcame his desire to get married. This Third Born turned off that anxiety by being angry with his fiancée. There was absolutely nothing wrong with the relationship other than his anxiety.

Many bachelors across the country are fearful Third Born types. These guys want to have a relationship, but because of their feelings of vulnerability, they avoid social situations where they might meet someone. They don't go to dances, weddings, or work parties. Heaven forbid they should actually have to talk with someone of the opposite sex.

One bachelor wanted desperately to meet a woman, but he spent all of his time with his parents. Now, there's a great way to meet women. That insulated him from meeting anyone other than the neighbor lady and the guy who delivered the mail.

One other eligible bachelor had a great idea. He ran an ad to meet a woman just before he went out of town for two weeks. Women responded to the ad, but since he wasn't around to follow up, nothing came of it. He was putting off responding to women because he felt vulnerable. He suffered from the horrible dilemma of wanting to meet women but being afraid to talk to them. This guy finally did meet a woman who was aggressive enough to insist on communicating with him, but she wasn't the kind of person he really wanted to marry. Guess what? This man is still single.

When a Third Born does have a close relationship, such as in a marriage, he or she seeks to please the partner rather than becoming close through honesty. Third Borns don't want anyone—even a spouse—to see their true feelings. That would make them about as vulnerable as a person could be. Third Borns hide their true feelings while doing for the other person what they believe the other person wants or appreciates.

It's much easier for a Third Born to spend an extra hour in the yard working on the bushes or flower garden because she or he knows that's the spouse will appreciate it than to sit down and have a conversation about how terrible work was that week, for example.

Third Borns may also sacrifice their own desires, goals, and preferences in order to please someone else. They please others until they feel empty themselves, at which point they may do something irrational in desperation to please themselves. For example, a Third Born mother who has been sacrificing her own interests in order to please her family may go gambling and spend more than the family can afford to fill that empty feeling.

If you happen to have a Third Born in the house, there's a good chance you have heard this phrase many, many times: "I am really bored." Third Borns feel the need to constantly keep busy, have novelty in their lives, and to make frequent changes. As a result, they make many unnecessary changes in their lives.

Until one mother was introduced to Birth Order Personality, she could not understand her Third Born daughter's need to constantly change the furniture in her bedroom. This same Third Born might spend a whole day with her family doing everything from hiking and having a picnic to playing baseball in a local park, and when everyone else in the family would get home and want a little space, a little time to do whatever they wanted to do, the Third Born would announce, "There's nothing to do. I'm bored."

Using her understanding of Birth Order Personality, this young girl's mother was able to talk to her daughter about the idea of being bored. She got her daughter to realize that reading a book or doing a crafts projects wasn't "boring" at all because the Third Born was actually doing something.

This little girl does love to be busy, and the whole family is learning how to channel this girl's energy and need for activity into something positive. This little girl sometimes gets up before everyone else and makes breakfast for the entire family. She pulls weeds in the yard. She writes books. Before you know it, she might be jacking up the house to add an extra layer of bricks to the basement.

Now that this Third Born's parents understand their daughter's need to always be doing something so she isn't bored, they are prepared to suggest activities for her and they love to hear the sound of her bedroom furniture moving across the floor. Life in their house is rarely boring.

Being busy, especially for older Third Borns, often just tends to cover up boredom rather than relieving it because their feelings of boredom are actually feelings of loneliness. Third Borns who have kept other people at a distance feel a sense of isolation from others, which would naturally make them feel lonely. But here's the catch: For Third Borns to admit to being lonely would arouse feelings of vulnerability, so they conveniently renamed the emotion boredom.

That doesn't stop Third Borns from engaging in frenetic activity to try and avoid boredom. They are often ready to set off on a new course of action if someone even mentions the idea of doing something else. A date with a Third Born could turn into a marathon. A Third Born wouldn't wait to just go out for a meal and talk; that would never be enough. This couple would get something to eat, take a walk, get dessert, go bowling, drive to the lake, stop for a snack, play tennis, go for a swim, and then go see a movie. Makes you tired just thinking about it doesn't it?

These Third Borns welcome interruptions in their day. They are happy when someone just "stops by," and they crave spontaneity in their relationships. They try to arrive a meetings exactly on time, because the unstructured time spent waiting can be boring. Also, this Birth Order Personality can often end up being late if they don't plan their schedule exactly to the minute.

Feelings of vulnerability can affect a Third Born at work, at play, or in relationships in various ways. One Third Born factory worker, for example, was valued by his supervisors because he not only showed great ability to do his tasks, but frequently came up with creative new ways to do the work more efficiently. Third Borns have a tendency to come up with great ideas, and fortunately for this worker, his supervisors listened to his ideas rather than telling him to write them up for the suggestion box. He would never have done that, because he needed to know that his ideas were pleasing to his superiors.

This man got along great with his coworkers. His "no problem" attitude was like a breath of fresh air to the men and women he worked with, and everyone thought he was a terrific worker and a great guy to be around. He also had a great sense of humor, which helps no matter which Birth Order you happened to slide into.

When it came time to fill a supervisor's position this man was a natural choice. He took the promotion but discovered very quickly that the new job gave him loads of anxiety. He began to feel vulnerable because he would now be a target for employee dissatisfaction.

Fortunately, this wise Third Born got therapy that enabled him to overcome his anxiety and continue in his new position. He was a superior supervisor, and everyone was happy for him. Three cheers for the Third Born.

Third Borns experience vulnerability as a feeling of being cornered. When they feel cornered, fear can drive them to try and fight their way out of the corner. As soon as the big fight is over, they stop being angry. Once in a great while, Third Borns who do not feel comfortable giving themselves permission to fight back may experience a psychotic breakdown. Rather than exploding with anger, they will experience a kind of psychological implosion.

Even though these Third Borns may attack, they do not have a true system of self-defense. They experience their lives as being a kind of public property, as if a "Free to a Good Home" sign had been permanently hung around their necks. These Third Borns are unable to speak up for themselves if someone invades their time, space, or personal possessions. They also have a hard time not answering personal, intrusive questions they really don't want to answer.

It's as if Third Borns are ready to have every truck in the world run over them. "Okay, here I am," the Third Born seems to be yelling at anyone who has garbage that needs to be thrown away. In therapy sessions with a Third Born, one of the first things a counselor does is to help the Third Born grow a defense system.

This sense of vulnerability does leave the Third Born with a tremendous gift. The Third Born Birth Order Personality has a tremendous amount of compassion for victims, as well as empathy for children, those who are developmentally disabled, the elderly, the poor, or anyone who needs help.

Third Borns often find ways to personally help people. Sometimes they drag home broken and discarded items that they plan to fix up and give to people who could not otherwise afford them. Third Borns' garages, basements and cupboards may be filled with this "stuff." They may end up sleeping on a tiny rug because the bed is covered with piles of clothing for the shelter and shoes they bought at a rummage sale for the next clothing drive. While their compassion is a more than admirable trait, Third Borns' behavior in this regard may also confuse the people who share their living space and who might not know that it stems from their Birth Order Personality.

Many Third Borns end up becoming nurses, but this group does not like working on the floor, where they have to take orders from the doctors. They prefer to be creatively compassionate in treating patients, rather than strictly following doctors' orders. The Third Born nurse would be happy to sneak in a patient's pet, or let a visitor stay late, or bring in the high school marching band if he or she thought it would help the patient recover.

Third Born nurses shine in the emergency room; this is their world. They thrive on crisis, and they love being able to react to the situation and not waiting to be told what to do. They are also able to express their sense of compassion to the fullest in this setting, comforting those needing emergency care. Their ability to act quickly in an emergency situation produces confidence in those needing help. The ever-changing, exciting, and challenging atmosphere of the ER also helps to keep away any thoughts of boredom, and the Third Born loves it.

Third Born nurses also do well in nursing homes. Their compassion enables them to relate to residents in comforting ways. Unlike in a hospital, where rules govern everything, their creativity is welcomed there. Most nursing homes will let a creative Third Born do whatever he or she can to help the residents. Third Borns can, however, get into trouble if they advocate for a patient against another nurse whom they feel is not treating patients compassionately.

While the cranky and cantankerous older patients can irritate some Birth Order Personalities, Third Born nurses love to help these people. It makes them happy when they can help others who are obviously unhappy, and they can't understand someone who doesn't feel the same way or is not willing to go the extra mile to make someone else feel good.

Third Borns generally have only one or two special friends. These friends give them an opportunity to bare their souls and to say exactly what they feel. They keep everyone else at arm's length, though they are friendly to many people. They choose their confidants carefully, based on how safe they feel with them.

This is a Birth Order filled with creative thinkers who often generate new ideas by making comparisons. One such Third Born, Lowell, was the pastor of a small town church. Since small towns are usually led by Second Borns, who like being a big fish in a small pond, Lowell's creative ideas were not much appreciated. The Second Borns wanted to keep everything just the way it was, which was why those Second Borns had never left the little pond in the first place: They could control everything in it. Thus, poor Lowell was not the most popular guy in town.

While he was trying to establish outreach programs and help groups of people who were normally overlooked, the Second Borns were angry with him because he was ignoring the church budget. They also didn't like the looks of the new people Lowell was bringing into the church.

Eventually, Lowell was transferred to an urban area. Here

he blossomed as a pastor. The fast-paced city life was just the ticket for this boredom-fearing Third Born. He worked like crazy to make the church prosper, and his natural selling ability brought people to church, got them involved, and made the programs work. Lowell had found himself a place where he could be happy as a Third Born.

Third Borns make terrific salespeople. One company manager who had nine salespeople scattered across the country asked each one of the their Birth Order, and guess what? Every single one was a Third Born.

A company is wise to hire Third Borns for its sales force, yet should think twice about promoting one to sales manager. The Third Born manager would expect others to be able to do what he or she can do without providing the proper input. The best sales manager would be a Fourth Born—the natural people manager—who may not be the best salesperson.

Third Borns love to write poetry that allows them to use similes, metaphors, and other forms of comparison. As inventors, they are most likely to create new products out of a combination of ideas. Thomas Edison was one such Third Born, the seventh of seven children.

The feelings of vulnerability that are a signature trait of Third Borns also affect the Fourth Born Birth Order. From the beginning, Third Borns are dying to get rid of their feelings of vulnerability, and what better way to do that than to pass off some of those feelings onto the Fourth Born child? Guess what? Third Borns get a break, and Fourth Borns get ready. It's your turn, Fourth Born Birth Order Personality.

Chapter Nine

Life Isn't Easy;
You Have to Try Hard:
The Fourth Born

Fourth Borns, Fourth Borns, Fourth Borns. I bet you thought we would never get here, but it's going to be worth the wait. Really, it is. You poor guys and gals. If ever there was a Birth Order that has been misunderstood, misdiagnosed, and misplaced it is the Fourth Born. Saddle up and get ready for an adventure that will thrill you and help you understand who you really are.

This Birth Order Personality is an analytical person who feels in his or her heart that life is a struggle and that trying hard and then harder is the key to everything. The Fourth Born seems to have the words "hard work" tattooed on the side of the brain. Fourth Borns work hard, are often withdrawn, and have a tendency to let their anger get the best of them.

Talk about a complex personality; Fourth Borns, you have
it all. Remember, this is a chance for you to look at yourself
in a new and fascinating way. You may not have all of the
Fourth Born traits and characteristics, but you will have some
of them. Understanding the bits and pieces that make you a
Fourth Born can truly help you to have a more productive
and happy life.

Think about that for a minute. If you know that your Birth
Order Personality pushes you in certain directions, don't you
want to know why and how that happens? It's intriguing and
exciting and a way for the entire world to see you in a new
and positive light.

Out of all the Birth Orders, Fourth Borns have been and
continue to be the least understood. No one but a Fourth
Born can really understand the inner workings of this
Personality. From day one, Fourth Borns appear to get lost
in the crowd. No one knows them. No one appears to care.
The Fourth Born has a lot to be angry about, and he or she
does get angry. Sometimes really angry—but not all Fourth
Borns display this characteristic to such an extreme.

Just as the rest of the world tries to understand Fourth
Borns, they struggle to try and understand themselves. If you
are already having trouble pinpointing a Fourth Born, that
comes as no surprise; Fourth Borns feel the same way.

Are you ready for some characteristics? Have at it. Keep
an open mind. Call up a friend who knows you. You can do
this. If five or more of these characteristics seem to fit you to
a "T," this is it. You are a Fourth Born Birth Order Personality.

Fourth Born Birth Order Personality Characteristics

- You have to try hard.
- You analyze everything from every angle.

- It seems to you that life has to be hard.
- You like to work hard.
- It seems as if no one understands you, so you just clam up.
- You try to avoid getting trapped.
- You are always getting left out.
- You feel that no one listens to you.
- You can get confused with what others are saying.
- You think you have to control your feelings.
- You tend to get suspicious when someone does something nice for you for no apparent reason.
- You notice when others are being lazy.
- You tend to withdraw at family gatherings.
- You wait for a special invitation before you join a group.
- You like to entertain others with your wit.

What a Birth Order Personality you are, Fourth Borns. Your life offers an interesting set of challenges that, from the outset, set you on the Fourth Born path of work, more work, and then a little bit of work for dessert.

The arrival of a Fourth Born in a family gives great joy to the Third Born. Finally, the Third Born Birth Order Personality has a place to dump his or her vulnerability, and that's right into the little lap of the Fourth Born brother or sister. Of course, there are also two other siblings to contend with, but the Fourth Born really needs to keep all eyes and ears on the Third Born.

In a Third Born's eyes, this little baby is already vulnerable. This baby is the youngest, can't do anything without anyone's help, and will have to rely on the older brothers and sisters to teach him or her the ways of the world. This is what gets a Third Born rejoicing and what a Fourth Born will come to dread.

While the baby is getting its bearings, it seems as if the

Third Born is thinking up ways to make the Fourth Born feel vulnerable, so he or she doesn't have to feel that way anymore. This happened in one family pretty darn fast.

A mother with Third and Fourth Born daughters was giving both of them a bath one day. The Third Born girl was four years old and the Fourth Born was just three months old. While Mom was busy with the soap and washcloth and making sure no one drowned or got soap in her eye, the Third Born kept up a running commentary on every single thing the Fourth Born did or did not do.

"You know she can't even splash in the water yet," reported the Third Born.

"Yes, that's true," said the mom, anxious to hear what was going to be said next.

"My little sister can't even stand up in the bathtub yet," said the Third Born.

"No, honey, she's just a baby," said Mom.

"Look, Mommy, she can't even hold a washcloth or anything yet."

"Well, sweetie, she's just a little baby."

"Yes, but she can't do anything, can she Mommy?"

Mom has her work cut out for her, and so does the Fourth Born. It the Third Born was so critical of her new sister as an infant, imagine what it was like the following year and the year after that? The Third Born was so anxious to pass on her vulnerable feelings that she pretty much started in on her new sibling from day one.

Fourth Borns who were unsure of their Birth Order Personality up to now may start feeling as if something has suddenly fallen into place. Remember the older sister always telling you that you were too little to play? How about the times when she told you that you didn't know anything because you were just a baby—or too young or too dumb or too short? Too anything in the whole world? Welcome to the challenging world of the Fourth Born Birth Order Personality.

You probably want a little more to go on before we jump into the days and nights in the life of a Fourth Born. Review the following Fourth Born Birth Order Personality traits and take your time when you think about them. Think objectively. As with all Birth Orders, you need to have at least five of these traits to be considered a good candidate for this Birth Order Personality.

Fourth Born Birth Order Personality Traits

- Feels excluded
- Feels immature
- Is analytical
- Is distrustful
- Uses retaliatory justice
- Does not listen to self
- Feels others do not listen
- Can be pushy or passive
- Is hard-working
- Controls feelings to control behavior
- Frequently harbors anger
- Is secretive
- Is sensitive to blame
- Uses insulting humor

How the Fourth Born Copes with Feelings of Immaturity

Fourth Borns definitely have a tough and long road to hoe, but that doesn't mean that their efforts won't pay off. All things are possible with understanding, patience, and, in the case of this Birth Order, lots of hard work.

As the Fourth Born begins to grow, the constant remarks

and not-so-fine treatment by the Third Born begin to make the Fourth Born feel as if he or she will never grow up. While the Third Born is busy trying to pass on some feelings of vulnerability, he or she also ends up making the Fourth Born feel immature. The Onlies, First, and Second Borns don't help much either. Comments such as, "Mom, do we have to take him along? He'll just slow us down" or "Let's leave the baby with Dad," can make the Fourth Born feel like there is no hope of ever getting or acting any older.

Some Fourth Borns never lose this feeling of immaturity, because they have given in to thinking that others appear more mature than they do. Other Fourth Borns become "super-mature" when they try to overcome the feeling of immaturity by being more mature than anyone else. These Fourth Borns are very reasonable, understanding, responsible, calm, supportive, attentive, and dependable. They tend to speak slowly. They are accepting of others regardless of what they have done, they suggest good ideas without forcing them on anyone else, and they are the kind of people you'd like to have around. Nevertheless, the feelings of immaturity are always there in the background, haunting them like a bad dream. This Birth Order can never let up on the drive to feel and appear mature.

Fourth Borns develop two major strategies for overcoming immaturity. The first strategy is developed as they watch older siblings doing things that would be difficult for them. As they watch, they decide that if they could accomplish these things they would be OK. It may be something as simple as doing homework or learning how to drive a car, or jogging three miles around the neighborhood lake. The Fourth Born would think, "Wow, as soon as I can do that, I am going to be grown up, and people will respect me."

This group of Fourth Borns craves the challenge of hard tasks and do not do things the easy way. If they did, well, they would never become mature. Life is hard; jobs have to be hard. We all have to work hard. That's how the Fourth Born thinks.

As they get older, these Fourth Borns are like little worker bees while on the job. They seem tireless. They work so hard they make others tired just looking at them. When they are at home they always have to be working on something, and it's almost impossible for them to relax. There is simply too much for this Fourth Born to do. There are miles and miles to go before they sleep—or, for that matter, even sit down.

If you ask Fourth Borns what they hate more than anything, guess what they will say? Laziness. It drives them crazy, and they feel as if the entire world should hate laziness as much as they do. But being lazy once in a while isn't so bad, is it? Hard work is rewarding, but so is sitting in the backyard, watching the birds build a nest and sipping a cold glass of lemonade.

Fourth Borns don't just work hard; they love to talk about working hard as well. In the back of their mind they are assuming that the listener is thinking, "This person must really be mature to be such a hard worker." This Birth Order Personality desperately wants you to think that hard work equals maturity. This is a very important issue to them. Even if they don't get much done, they love to talk about how hard they tried to work.

Can you remember ever hearing someone give a speech like the following? If you are a Fourth Born, maybe you have even done so yourself: "Man, I worked my butt off today, and it was like an uphill battle but I never gave up. Everyone else left early, but I, of course, stayed late. Didn't get much done, but, hey, I was there all by myself." That's our Fourth Born. You can't fault them for giving the world every good intention in the book.

Some of these Fourth Borns take a different angle when it comes to talking about work. Instead of talking about how hard they work, they complain about the difficulties they face every day while they are trying to get the job done. They imagine that the complaining is a good way to show the world how mature they are. They don't just complain about work, either. They like to do it about everything.

For example, if a Fourth Born happened to end up in the hospital, he or she would have a million things to complain about, in addition to the reason for being there in the first place: the food, the nurses, the size of the bed, the fact that there's no window, the unfriendly person in the next bed, or a lack of visitors would all be causes for finding fault. These Fourth Borns don't really expect anybody to do anything about all these problems, they just want someone to appreciate all they are enduring.

Some Fourth Borns take the opposite approach when it comes to complaining: They wouldn't complain if their life depended on it. To them, suffering in silence is proof of their maturity. You could offer this Fourth Born the moon or a winning lottery ticket if he or she gave you an honest appraisal of how bad a situation might be, but the Fourth Born would not do it.

The second strategy that Fourth Borns use to escape the immaturity that they imagine makes them unacceptable to others is to dissociate from themselves. They think that if they could just get away from themselves, they would be fine. This is not an easy concept to grasp, but Fourth Borns will know exactly what this means: simply put, it means that they don't listen to themselves. They think that by ignoring their inner voices, the thoughts and feelings that make them who they are, they will be a better, more mature person. So they stop listening to themselves, looking at themselves, and being themselves.

This type of thinking—or nonthinking, depending on how you look at it—creates lots of confusion for the Fourth Borns. This confusion can become magnified when a Fourth Born is under stress. All of us need to talk with ourselves in order to process information. "Let's see, it's cold out, I better get a sweater," or "That man really doesn't seem to be interested in me, so I might as well forget about it" are two fairly simple examples of how we talk to ourselves and process what happens around us.

Imagine a person humming to try and ignore what is happening and you get an idea of how some Fourth Borns try to block out their thoughts. Because they try not to listen to themselves, their minds become cloudy during times when they need to think clearly to get from point A to point B.

Because Fourth Borns do not listen to themselves, they end up being totally confused when they are at odds with someone in conversation or during times of stress when communicating with one's inner self is very important. If a Fourth Born is in a counseling session, for example, he might react in confusion to the challenge of the counseling by throwing up his hands, saying, "I can't take it," and walking out of the room.

The immature-type Fourth Borns may experience problems talking with others. It can be very hard for them to develop an inner response because they cannot listen to themselves while they are listening to someone else. For example, a man "listening" to his wife had nothing to say when she finished talking. She had made some significant points, but he did not "hear" any response in himself to what she said, so he was speechless when it was his turn to talk.

The super-mature Fourth Borns hear both themselves and others. These Fourth Borns may not respond immediately because they take the time to hear themselves. When they do reply, their responses are appropriate, thoughtful, and reasonable.

Many Fourth Borns feel that no one understands them—which is actually true and makes a lot of sense, since the Fourth Born does not understand him- or herself. It's tough to understand how and why a Fourth Born thinks and acts. When someone does show some understanding of a Fourth Born, the Fourth Born will open up.

It is also very tough for Fourth Borns to take feedback. When faced with criticism, they often react with anger, blame someone else, or simply clam up. One Fourth Born was having a conversation with his wife and other family members at a family reunion recently. A few of his cousins and uncles began kidding him, half seriously, about the weight he was beginning to carry about the middle section of his body. The Fourth Born took the kidding for a moment and then, as if someone has turned on a switch, suddenly became very angry. He started defending himself by saying that he was too busy to work out and that he was getting a little older so it was okay for him to gain weight. Then he turned to his wife and shouted in front of everyone. "This is your fault, you know. If you weren't such a good cook and always making me big meals, then this would never have happened to me."

The relatives were stunned at this outburst, but his wife was not. In fact, she had been trying to get out of the conversation because she knew that, sooner or later, someone was going to get it. Unfortunately, that someone ended up being her.

Another Fourth Born who worked in a large office knew that she had not been doing her job the way she was supposed to do it. She had forgotten to do some of her assigned tasks and was generally slacking off in all areas. When the supervisor called her into the office and asked, "What are you going to do about it?" in an attempt to make the Fourth Born accountable for her actions, the Fourth Born blew up and ran out.

Fourth Borns just have a hard time being themselves. Right from the get-go, all of their older siblings pushed them around, so naturally it was hard to be true to themselves.

Things didn't get much better as they got older, as all their brothers and sisters continued to boss them around. As a result, Fourth Borns often lost track of who they were. To regain their identities, Fourth Borns may "borrow" one from someone else. Just like a chameleon that adapts its color to its surroundings, Fourth Borns adapt their personality. One good way to think of this is to imagine a Fourth Born watching a movie. The Fourth Born will focus on a specific character in the movie, becoming totally absorbed in thinking about how it would feel to be that character.

In counseling sessions Fourth Borns who are confronted with the complexities of their behavior will often respond, "Well, how am I supposed to act?" It is much easier for them to take behavioral cues from the counselor than to take a look inside themselves and be who they are really supposed to be.

The Fourth Born's dissociation from themselves causes some psychologists and psychiatrists to diagnose them as having a multiple personality disorder. Some Fourth Borns eagerly accept that idea, as it gives them a really good reason for not being themselves.

This, of course, is a pretty extreme case. Very few Fourth Borns get this far in trying to remove themselves from themselves, so to speak. Those who have given up their identities, however, have a very hard time feeling empathetic or giving sympathy. Since they do not have an identity to make them feel guilty, they do not feel guilty when hurting someone else. Neither do they feel compassion for someone who is sick. A Fourth Born husband, for example, might ask his wife, who has been in bed with the flu all day, to get up and make him some dinner.

Stay calm, Fourth Borns. You are not headed toward becoming an insensitive heap of humanity. These are extreme cases. The majority of Fourth Borns have hearts of gold; they are sensitive and would feel guilty if they caused anyone to feel bad or uneasy. The world is full of these nice Fourth Borns who are untroubled by severe identity problems.

Additional Fourth Born Attitudes and Behaviors

In fact, because of their wonderful ability to deal with people, Fourth Borns are often able to resolve difficult situations. One Fourth Born pastor discovered that the church treasurer had embezzled some money from the church, and instead of having the embezzler arrested or coming down hard on him himself, the pastor found a way for the man to make restitution and save his career and his family life. He also helped the man get some professional help, so he would see where he had made the wrong choices. By having the man stand up in front of the entire congregation and admit that he had made mistakes, the pastor was also able to motivate his other parishioners to be supportive of the man, to forgive him, and to use what happened as a positive experience for the church. This pastor used his natural management skills in a manner that not only helped the man in question, but set an example for hundreds of other people.

Many Fourth Borns are also great management thinkers. They can look at a situation and accurately judge what needs to be done to make it better. One seventeen-year-old boy was eating pizza in a restaurant with a friend who observed that this Fourth Born was taking mental notes on what was happening in the restaurant as they were having dinner.

"What are you thinking about?" the man asked his young friend.

"I'm just thinking that this place could be run a lot better," said the Fourth Born.

"Don't you like it here?"

"Sure, it's okay, but I just think things could be made more efficient and just better all around," said the boy.

"Have you ever worked in a restaurant?"

"Nope."

"How do you know then?" asked the man, who had some knowledge of Birth Order Personality and could tell that this boy was thinking just like a Fourth Born.

"It just makes sense to me to put the kitchen in a different area, to make certain they have enough workers on the floor, and to put that one guy with all the experience behind the counter."

There you have it; a budding Fourth Born restaurant manager who has never delivered a pizza to a table in his life. When Fourth Borns are in touch with who they are, they are terrific analytical thinkers. They have the capacity to look at life in many different ways.

Many Fourth Borns who take the trouble to understand who they are and what they think and feel are some of the most wonderful people on the face of the earth. One Fourth Born man from Iowa struggled his whole life with terrible feelings that he did not understand. This man—we'll call him Bob—spent most of his life in what he calls a "rage" and he had no idea why.

"The littlest things would upset me to the point of violence," said Bob. "I'm a very good wall smasher, and absolutely anything at all could set me off."

Twice married and divorced, Bob says that he knows now that all he needed was some understanding and the ability to let his emotions flow in a positive manner. He said he had always thought people didn't really care about him—a classic Fourth Born trait—and because of that those marriages ended up failing.

"Everything was confusing for me, and I would just end up in fits of rage because I didn't know what else to do," remembers Bob. "I would keep myself from crying, because

I felt that men don't cry and that I was being mature by acting that way."

Bob struggled for years. He was verbally abusive to both his wives and can't remember ever being happy—but he wanted to be happy. He wanted to be able to smile and to enjoy life. He said counseling using Birth Order helped him learn who he was and gave him an understanding of himself so that he could understand others.

"Now that I am in a wonderful relationship, I look back and think that I was stressed out all the time because I never knew what to do or who I was," said Bob. "I'm having a blast with life now, and I can tell you that Fourth Borns don't have to feel the way they do."

Bob, like many people who have studied Birth Order, says that he can now pick out Fourth Borns all over the place.

"Fourth Borns always think that no one listens or cares, because they spend their lives feeling ignored," said Bob. "That's a big part of who we are."

This isn't a simple process, is it? Imagine how the Fourth Born feels and you may look at the world differently. Once you understand these concepts, it's as if a light goes on and you can see why certain people do the things they do. It happens all the time. Fourth Borns are pretty wonderful, just like those Onlies and First, Second, and Third Borns. All of us have a little bit of the good, the bad, and the ugly.

Fourth Borns who have a positive outlook on life really want to make things easier for others by taking more on themselves. This is one way for them to develop a sense of maturity. They can face difficulty, be strong, be mature, and give others a break from the serious side of life. There is a type of Fourth Born who is "super-mature." These Fourth Borns are not easy to identify because they do not show the signs of anger, immaturity, or vengefulness. Rather, they behave in an unusually mature fashion.

A super-mature Fourth Born parent reasons with a misbehaving child. Picture this: the child has done something wrong. The father lovingly puts his arm around the child's shoulders, explains how the behavior was wrong, how it hurt others in the family, and what the child can do to make restitution. The child is restored into relationship rather than punished.

A super-mature Fourth Born seems to never get angry. The immature Fourth Born, on the other hand, can be angry all the time. A super-mature Fourth Born may turn to mystical religion to deal with the injustices of life while the immature Fourth Born turns to force, physical or emotional.

In a family setting, siblings may depend on the super-mature Fourth Born to deal with family issues, even though other siblings are older. In the work place, the super-mature Fourth Born is the manager who can get the employees to perform well without having to pressure them.

The immature-type Fourth Born is another story. They are often easy to identify. They are pushy, aggressive, and bold. They can be embarrassing to be with if something is not to their liking—in a restaurant, for example. One Fourth Born woman decided from the moment she walked into the restaurant where she was meeting some friends that she didn't like the place. She sent her food back three times, complained about her wine, and ended up getting her meal for free. Her friends were mortified by her behavior, but the Fourth Born thought she had really scored a great deal.

Another immature Fourth Born was able to get custody of his children in the midst of a messy divorce by sheer force. He broke into his ex-wife's house, and as he was doing so, a policeman arrived. This Fourth Born waved an official looking paper at the officer saying, "I have a court order." The policeman did not look at the piece of paper, which was actually a rent receipt, and the man absconded with his sons. The wife, who was terrified to go against this Fourth Born, backed down from the custody battle and let him keep the boys.

In another case, a Fourth Born man broke into his girlfriend's house, abused her, tore the phone off the wall, and
then pushed her down the basement steps. When the police
showed up, the Fourth Born told them that the woman had
called him, and that when he had showed up at the door,
she had been screaming and would not answer it. He told
them he had broken into the house to make sure she was
all right and had discovered that the phone had been ripped
off the wall. He said the woman had run screaming down
the basement steps at hearing him break in and had fallen.
Fortunately, the police in this case knew the Fourth Born
was lying.

This is a great example of a Fourth Born using his analytical thinking to create a believable story. Some Fourth
Borns, in fact, get away with lying because they do it with
some wonderful details. One Fourth Born, for example, said
he had to go settle an argument between a woman and her
boyfriend because her father was upset about it. The whole
story was a fabrication but seemed believable because of the
additional detail about the father being upset.

Analytical thinking, like any Personality trait, can either
be used for something positive or something negative. The
young boy in the pizza restaurant was using his Fourth Born
powers constructively, while the guys who lied to the police
officers were headed in the opposite direction.

One of the most easily identifiable Fourth Born
Personality traits is an aversion to feeling used. Fourth Borns
hate to feel as if someone is taking advantage of them, and
they are very mindful of not letting it happen.

If a Fourth Born child is standing around at the playground
waiting for someone to ask him or her to join in and is suddenly asked to chase down a ball, he or she will not want
to do it. The Fourth Born will think, "What's in it for me?"
If the Fourth Born is not playing the game, well, forget about
it. This feeling can and often does carry over into adulthood.

If Fourth Borns do not feel as if they are getting something out of a specific action or situation, they are going to feel as if they are being used.

It's also important to remember that Fourth Borns hate the idea of being trapped. This feeling is closely related to feeling used because being used is also a trap—Get the ball, please, but you can't play with us. Fourth Borns stay on the lookout for other situations where they might be forced—at least in their minds—into something they don't want to do.

The fear of being trapped can grow to such an extent that it develops into a kind of paranoia that predisposes Fourth Borns to look at anything good done for them as a potential trap. If you have a friend who is a Fourth Born and you volunteer to pick up a gallon of milk for that person, he or she may spend of great deal of time wondering, "What is she getting out of this?"

Fourth Borns can actually end up feeling angry if someone does something nice for them. Bring home some flowers for a Fourth Born and you might hear, "Why did you do that? Why did you spend all that money on flowers? Are you trying to make up for something you did wrong?"

This phenomenon might help to explain why, when the wife of an abusive Fourth Born husband tries to do nice things for him, she ends up getting treated even worse than usual because her actions make the Fourth Born feel trapped, and thus angry.

One Fourth Born daughter spent years striking back at her mother and father for their acts of generosity. They gave her money and helped her and her struggling family move. They bought them a refrigerator when they could not afford one and came each and every time this Fourth Born daughter needed help. Their reward? Anger. This woman would yell at her parents, never say thank you and spend weeks not responding to their phone calls. In the back of her mind, this Fourth Born was always wondering what her parents were going to ask her to do in return. She wanted and needed help, but was angry when she got it and could never seem to get beyond this point.

This sense of feeling trapped leaves Fourth Borns no escape, so they feel that all they can do is retaliate. This daughter, for example, ended up spreading rumors about her own parents. She told her siblings how terrible they were and tried to get her aunts and uncles to hate them. Like many Fourth Borns, this woman felt as if she had nothing to lose by retaliating for the sense of anger her parents inadvertently caused her to feel. She felt hopeless, trapped, and angry.

Some Fourth Borns take this anger as far as it will go, feeling as if they have nothing to lose and that getting even is the only thing to do. These thoughts may end up with the Fourth Born committing a murderous crime that is completely justified in his or her mind.

Remember the Betty Broderick story? It made national headlines and became a television movie. This woman shot and killed her ex-husband and his new wife while they were sleeping, but got off with a second-degree murder conviction. The first trial ended with a hung jury. The story that almost got her off was that she was so upset by her husband getting the children and leaving her without the financial resources she was accustomed to, she was going to kill herself.

Her story was mesmerizing. She said that she had taken her gun to the beach to shoot herself, but that once she had gotten there, she had instead decided to punish her husband for changing her life. For causing her such pain. For ruining everything she had. She was going to punish him by shooting herself in front of him. Then he would feel guilty.

Broderick went to her husband's house and let herself in with a key she had made, walked up the stairs to his bedroom, and stood at the edge of the bed. She said that her husband moved suddenly and her gun went off in reaction, killing both him and his wife.

It is easy to see how the jury was swayed by this story. We can all empathize with how bad she must have felt at the circumstances her husband left her in. Betty Broderick knew how to read people and how to tell her story so that the jurors would feel and see and hear the same things that she had.

One easy way to pick out a Fourth Born is to see how he or she handles social gatherings. Fourth Borns often don't feel as if anyone wants them around, as when they were babies and pushed around by the other kids in the family. They don't feel welcome in groups and don't like to join clubs or organizations. They really need a special invitation to feel wanted.

If you watch Fourth Borns at a social gathering, you will see that they like to be off by themselves and do something like watch television or play with the children while everyone else is visiting. They also may become the family entertainer, as the children love the attention, which makes the Fourth Born in turn feel wanted. The Fourth Born will also feel wanted if he or she can make everyone laugh, tell a few great stories, or do something special to get everyone's attention.

Fourth Borns aren't surprised by the fact that their families seem to forget about them as adults. Ask almost any Fourth Born to give you an example of this, and he or she will come up with dozens of stories. In one family, for example, everyone—including the mother—forgot to tell the Fourth Born son that his father had had a heart attack and was in the intensive care unit of the local hospital.

Can you imagine being in this situation? Probably not, if you are any Birth Order Personality other than a Fourth Born. After this poor guy was missed in the phone calling chain, the family forgot him again when the doctor came in to discuss the health of the father. The Fourth Born was sitting alone in the next room.

One woman, who was notified that her elderly brother had passed away immediately began calling everyone in her family. She called her children, her nieces, and her neighbors. Yet, she totally forgot to call her Fourth Born daughter. "She does this all the time," said the Fourth Born. "You would think that I would get used to it, but I never do. It still bothers me. I'm a grown woman and my family is still amazed that I know how to set the table."

The Fourth Born is the forgotten person. This is not just true in family settings, but in the professional world of psychology as well. Only four personalities are usually identified in psychological tests, and the Fourth Born is once again left out in the cold. *The Birth Order Effect* is the only place where a Fourth Born can actually learn about his or her specific personality.

This is actually the first time a description of a Fourth Born Personality has been made widely available. No one understands the Fourth Born, because no one had to understand him or her while growing up. The older children could overpower the Fourth Born, so there was no need to come to an understanding of him or her.

Fourth Borns, on the other hand, had plenty of time to figure out who they were dealing with. As a child, the Fourth Born had to deal with a whole set of siblings, and all of their various Personalities, so the Fourth Born had to figure them out in order to survive. On a basic level, Fourth Borns can understand almost everybody but Onlies.

Since this Birth Order knows that no one understands them, they have a hard time opening up. Because Fourth Borns are not "joiners," it has been fairly impossible for them to be studied by those who explore personality behavior, which is usually looked at in groups.

As Cliff Isaacson began developing his ideas on Birth Order Personalities, he was unable to unravel the interesting Fourth Born mind and heart until some of his Fourth Born clients began taking the risk of sharing information about themselves and their feelings. These Birth Order discoveries

have already helped thousands of people, and there are millions more Fourth Borns who would benefit from learning
how and why they function as they do.

In looking at Fourth Born marriages, it is evident that the
Fourth Born often picks a spouse who is either years younger
or older. There may be five or more years' difference in age.
A Fourth Born man who feels immature may subconsciously
seek a much younger woman to match his feelings of immaturity. Sometimes a Fourth Born man seeks a woman who is
much older than himself because it helps him to feel more
mature. A Fourth Born woman may marry an older or
younger man for the same reasons.

See, Fourth Borns? You thought you were just like
everyone else. Hardly. Each and every Birth Order Personality
has its own fascinating ins and outs. This amazing way of
looking at personality really is the key to understanding and
more positive personal relationships.

So what happens when the next kid comes along? This
is a fairly easy scenario. When the fifth child comes on the
scene, the Fourth Born ignores him or her, hoping with all
his or her heart to be able to pass on the feeling of being
unwanted. Instead, the fifth child feels immediately like an
Only Child and this wonderful Birth Order process starts all
over again.

Simply the thing that I am
shall make me live.
—William Shakespeare

Chapter Ten

So You Think the Only Thing Your Father Gave You Were His Bright Blue Eyes? Secondary Birth Order Characteristics

No matter how hard we try, we can't seem to get away from our genetic beginnings. It's no coincidence that we have our father's bald spot, our mother's large eyes, or that wicked laugh of Grandma Smith's we remember hearing when we were growing up.

It would make sense, then, that we might also be getting just a bit more than that. How true it is, and how wonderful, that elements of both our insides and outsides are quiet gifts from the people who helped bring us into the world.

Our own Birth Order Personality was influenced by our parents and our relationship with them. As a basis for understanding this, let's first review some of what you now know.

Remember that in this book we have done away with the

old system of determining personality based on chronological birth order. There is no "middle child," and Birth Order Personality is applicable to as many children as a family can hold, since the cycle of Birth Order Personality continuously repeats itself. Gender has nothing to do with it. Moreover, your older siblings have nothing over you when it comes to Birth Order Personality, and if you cruise through *The Birth Order Effect* before they do, you will knock their socks off at the next family gathering.

Birth Order Personality and Secondary Characteristics

Variety in the expression of Birth Order Personality results from secondary characteristics that we inherit from our parents—the people who raised us. These secondary characteristics interact with our Birth Order Personality in positive ways to produce behavior, but they usually become submerged when we are under stress. When the going gets rough, our primary Birth Order Personality traits become dominant.

When it comes to inherited traits, there is definitely more than meets the eye—our parental gifts go way beyond our long fingers, flat feet, and those bright blue eyes. This may seem complicated at first, but the following rules of secondary characteristics and charts should help you. Sometimes it helps to try and digest just one idea at a time. If your head is starting to hurt, take a walk around the neighborhood before moving on to the next section. Your heart and your head will thank you.

Rules of Secondary Characteristics

Early in Cliff Isaacson's experience in working with Birth Order, he discovered that during friendly conversations, people often exhibit a different Birth Order Personality than when they are under stress. This raised the question of how people seemed to have more than one Birth Order Personality. This puzzle was solved by correlating these Birth Order Personalities in amiable circumstances to the Birth Order Personalities of the parents or those who raised the children. It appeared that the parental Birth Order Personalities created secondary Birth Order Personalities in the children. In stressful situations these secondary personalities would be set aside for the primary Birth Order Personality. In other words, the secondary personalities did not provide the coping strategies but did contribute to the personality in other ways.

> "Knowledge is never useless."
> —Anonymous

It is the primary Birth Order characteristics of parents that create the secondary Birth Order characteristics in children. The parents exhibited these primary characteristics when they were under stress, and therefore passed them on to their children.

Cliff Isaacson isolated specific rules governing how these secondary Birth Order Personalities are created in children. They are as follows:

1. Secondary characteristics are inherited from one's parents. Each person can have up to two secondary Personalities—one from each parent.
2. Secondary characteristics interact with primary characteristics to produce behavior.
3. Many people tend to focus on their secondary characteristics as opposed to their primary characteristics. This sometimes makes it difficult to quickly determine a correct Birth Order Personality.
4. An Only Child inherits the Birth Order characteristics of both parents. For example, an Only Child with a Second

Born mother and a Third Born father will have both the Second and Third Born secondary Birth Order Personality characteristics.

5. All other Birth Orders inherit one of their secondary Birth Order Personalities directly from the parent of the opposite sex. A First Born daughter would take on her father's Second Born Birth Order Personality as her secondary trait. A Second Born son with a Third Born mother would inherit the Third Born Birth Order Personality as a secondary trait.

6. All Birth Orders, except the Only Child, take on the Birth Order Personality that follows the Personality of the parent of the same sex as their second secondary Personality. For example, a First Born girl with a Second Born mother will take on a Third Born Birth Order Personality as a secondary characteristic. A son with a Second Born father will take on Third Born Personality traits as secondary characteristics.

7. All Birth Orders take on Only Child characteristics from an Only Child parent of either sex. All Birth Orders except the Only Child inherit Only Child characteristics from the Fourth Born parent of the same sex.

8. During times of stress, our primary Birth Order characteristics take over. At other times, those secondary characteristics kick in.

9. A life partner is usually chosen based on the Birth Order of a parent of the same sex. The partner will tend to be either of the same or the next Birth Order Personality as that parent.

Are you really confused now? You must be an Only Child. Just kidding. Remember, have fun with this and it will stick to your brain cells much easier. The following chart should help you see how this works.

Secondary Characteristics

In the following chart, superscript numbers and the superscript letter O represent secondary characteristics. Remember that most people have two secondary birth orders, so be sure to check both charts.

Mother	*Children*
Only Child	Sons: O^0, 1^0, 2^0, 3^0, 4^0
	Daughters: O^0, 1^0, 2^0, 3^0, 4^0
First	Sons: O^1, 1^1, 2^1, 3^1, 4^1
	Daughters: O^1, 1^2, 2^2, 3^2, 4^2
Second	Sons: O^2, 1^2, 2^2, 3^2, 4^2
	Daughters: O^2, 1^3, 2^3, 3^3, 4^3
Third	Sons: O^3, 1^3, 2^3, 3^3, 4^3
	Daughters: O^3, 1^4, 2^4, 3^4, 4^4
Fourth	Sons: O^4, 1^4, 2^4, 3^4, 4^4
	Daughters: O^4, 1^0, 2^0, 3^0, 4^0

Father	*Children*
Only Child	Daughters: O^0, 1^0, 2^0, 3^0, 4^0
	Sons: O^0, 1^0, 2^0, 3^0, 4^0
First	Daughters: O^1, 1^1, 2^1, 3^1, 4^1
	Sons: O^1, 1^2, 2^2, 3^2, 4^2
Second	Daughters: O^2, 1^2, 2^2, 3^2, 4^2
	Sons: O^2, 1^3, 2^3, 3^3, 4^3
Third	Daughters: O^3, 1^3, 2^3, 3^3, 4^3
	Sons: O^3, 1^4, 2^4, 3^4, 4^4
Fourth	Daughters: O^4, 1^4, 2^4, 3^4, 4^4
	Sons: O^4, 1^0, 2^0, 3^0, 4^0

As you progress through the book and study the various Birth Order Personality traits, the concept of secondary characteristics should begin to fall into place. For example, if you discover that you have inherited some Second Born secondary characteristics from your mother, it might help explain why you try to be perfect most of the time, but when you are really, really busy, you don't seem to care so much about details.

One First Born woman with a Third Born mother had Fourth Born secondary characteristics that led her to work hard—not for the sake of working hard in itself, as most Fourth Borns do, but for the sake of her goals, which were important to her as a First Born. Because her father was a Second Born, she also became a perfectionist—not for its own sake, as some Second Borns tend to be, but in order to make others think well of her, in characteristic First Born behavior.

Get it? You will. Hang in there. It's quite a voyage of discovery. Let the scenery soak in a bit before you start worrying about the destination.

Although Isaacson continues to discover the effects of secondary characteristics, he has already made some amazing related discoveries via his work with numerous clients.

For example, he has found that so called "ladies' men" are usually Onlies with secondary Third Born characteristics inherited from their mothers. These men tend to be successful—not only in their relations with women, but also in careers, business, and politics. They are usually very personable, which makes them attractive to women. One such man told Isaacson that he had a special trick he would use at dances: He would simply dance with all the women there at one time or another because he thought everyone deserved to be asked to dance at least once. While the tendency of other guys to focus specifically on the women they are interested in may backfire, because those women may perceive them as predatory, this smart guy caught the eye of lots of women, who saw that he was being kind to everyone.

Isaacson also discovered that entrepreneurs tend to be First Borns with Third Born secondary characteristics. The goal-oriented behavior of the First Born combined with the Third Born's desire to please others can lead to a wish to start something new. If this person gets into the right kind of business—something that provides a service to people—they usually will do quite well. Isaacson himself is a First Born with Third Born secondary characteristics, and his entrepreneurial spirit helped him start his counseling center. In doing something he loved that at the same time helped others, he found a perfect fit.

The following list describes some fascinating results of the mingling of secondary characteristics with our primary birth Order characteristics and should give you an idea of how the combination of the two can affect your own life.

Secondary Characteristics: Effects on a Daughter

Only Child with Only Child mom	Is organized, and expects others to be organized
Only Child with Only Child dad	Feels good about being organized
Only Child with First Born mom	Worries about what might happen
Only Child with First Born dad	Is a goal-oriented organizer
Only Child with Second Born mom	Is a detailed organizer
Only Child with Second Born dad	Is shy
Only Child with Third Born mom	Is anxious
Only Child with Third Born dad	Is a creative organizer
Only Child with Fourth Born mom	Tries hard to be organized
Only Child with Fourth Born dad	Is disorganized

(continued)

Secondary Characteristics: Effects on a Daughter *(continued)*

First Born with Only Child mom	Is limited in the pursuit of goals
First Born with Only Child dad	Is organized in the pursuit of goals
First Born with First Born mom	Competes with others to reach goals
First Born with First Born dad	Dreams of doing great things
First Born with Second Born mom	Is quiet about goals
First Born with Second Born dad	Rejects goals internally
First Born with Third Born mom	Tries hard to impress others
First Born with Third Born dad	Pursues goals creatively
First Born with Fourth Born mom	Goal is to convince others
First Born with Fourth Born dad	Is an aggressive controller
Second Born with Only Child mom	Is confident
Second Born with Only Child dad	Competes emotionally
Second Born with First Born mom	Dethrones others
Second Born with First Born dad	Displays goal-oriented perfectionism
Second Born with Second Born mom	Competes by perfection
Second Born with Second Born dad	Is a super-perfectionist
Second Born with Third Born mom	Is defensive
Second Born with Third Born dad	Is a creative perfectionist
Second Born with Fourth Born mom	Is compliant
Second Born with Fourth Born dad	Works hard at trying to attain perfection

(continued)

Secondary Characteristics: Effects on a Daughter *(continued)*

Third Born with Only Child mom	Is social
Third Born with Only Child dad	Feels controlled
Third Born with First Born mom	Is assertive
Third Born with First Born dad	Is independent
Third Born with Second Born mom	Is confident
Third Born with Second Born dad	Is rationally creative
Third Born with Third Born mom	Is confidently creative
Third Born with Third Born dad	Is super creative
Third Born with Fourth Born mom	Is cautious
Third Born with Fourth Born dad	Tries hard to be creative

Fourth Born with Only Child mom	Works quietly
Fourth Born with Only Child dad	Struggles mentally
Fourth Born with First Born mom	Feels overpowered
Fourth Born with First Born dad	Perseveres toward goals
Fourth Born with Second Born mom	Is persuasive
Fourth Born with Second Born dad	Is an adamant perfectionist
Fourth Born with Third Born mom	Has a mystical bent
Fourth Born with Third Born dad	Tries hard creatively
Fourth Born with Fourth Born mom	Is confident
Fourth Born with Fourth Born dad	Is independent

Secondary Characteristics: Effects on a Son

Only Child with Only Child dad	Is organized, and expects others to be organized
Only Child with Only Child mom	Feels good about being organized
Only Child with First Born dad	Worries about what might happen
Only Child with First Born mom	Is a goal-oriented organizer
Only Child with Second Born dad	Is a detailed organizer
Only Child with Second Born mom	Is shy
Only Child with Third Born dad	Is anxious
Only Child with Third Born mom	Is a creative organizer
Only Child with Fourth Born dad	Tries hard to be organized
Only Child with Fourth Born mom	Is disorganized

First Born with Only Child dad	Is limited in the pursuit of goals
First Born with Only Child mom	Is organized in the pursuit of goals
First Born with First Born dad	Competes with others to reach goals
First Born with First Born mom	Dreams of doing great things
First Born with Second Born dad	Is quiet about goals
First Born with Second Born mom	Rejects goals internally
First Born with Third Born dad	Tries hard to impress others
First Born with Third Born mom	Pursues goals creatively
First Born with Fourth Born dad	Goal is to convince others
First Born with Fourth Born mom	Is an aggressive controller

(continued)

Secondary Characteristics: Effects on a Son (continued)

Second Born with Only Child dad	Is confident
Second Born with Only Child mom	Competes emotionally
Second Born with First Born dad	Dethrones others
Second Born with First Born mom	Displays goal-oriented perfectionism
Second Born with Second Born dad	Competes by perfection
Second Born with Second Born mom	Is a super-perfectionist
Second Born with Third Born dad	Is defensive
Second Born with Third Born mom	Is a creative perfectionist
Second Born with Fourth Born dad	Is compliant
Second Born with Fourth Born mom	Works hard at trying to attain perfection
Third Born with Only Child dad	Is social
Third Born with Only Child mom	Feels controlled
Third Born with First Born dad	Is assertive
Third Born with First Born mom	Is independent
Third Born with Second Born dad	Is confident
Third Born with Second Born mom	Is rationally creative
Third Born with Third Born dad	Is confidently creative
Third Born with Third Born mom	Is super-creative
Third Born with Fourth Born dad	Is cautious
Third Born with Fourth Born mom	Tries hard to be creative

Secondary Characteristics: Effects on a Son *(continued)*

Fourth Born with Only Child dad	Works quietly
Fourth Born with Only Child mom	Struggles mentally
Fourth Born with First Born dad	Feels overpowered
Fourth Born with First Born mom	Perseveres toward goals
Fourth Born with Second Born dad	Is persuasive
Fourth Born with Second Born mom	Adamant perfectionist
Fourth Born with Third Born dad	Has a mystical bent
Fourth Born with Third Born mom	Tries hard creatively
Fourth Born with Fourth Born dad	Is confident
Fourth Born with Fourth Born mom	Is independent

While secondary characteristics are an important part of who we are, the big picture is still created by our primary Birth Order traits. As you dissect yourself, however, you will begin to notice when specific secondary traits surface. If, for example, you find yourself repeating certain behaviors of your mother's or father's, there is a very good chance that their secondary characteristics are alive and pumping through your veins.

While none of us are looking for an excuse to blame someone else for who we have become or what we do, it is a comfort to know how the seeds of who we are were planted. Isn't it heartening to realize that you can get to know yourself a bit better?

Chapter Eleven

Trying a Birth Order
On for Size:
T-shirts for Everyone

Finding oneself in a specific Birth Order is not always easy. And with secondary characteristics bumping into our primary characteristics, many of us will see bits and pieces of ourselves in each Birth Order Personality. That's no reason for alarm, and something that trained psychologists and therapists who use Birth Order in their counseling deal with all the time.

While some may find their Birth Order Personality to be obvious, others may find it a chore to try and sort through the layers of life that have brought them to this point and figure out where they belong. Moreover, some people's Birth Order Personality may be mild if they grew up in a very stable, secure, and loving home, where there would be less of a need to develop strong coping strategies. Many people fit into this category. There are still plenty of *Leave It to Beaver* homes left in the world. Some parents really are pretty close to being perfect, and many people have had siblings who were fun to be with and treated them like an equal. Some of the Birth Order traits will not be as obvious in people who come from a home like this, but they will be there—and you'll know it.

In those homes where life was not as rosy, Birth Order was probably more influenced by what children in these families had to cope with. When life at home is hard, there is a tendency to develop distinct Birth Order characteristics.

Imagine for a minute, a Fourth Born who really was ignored and put down as a child and almost shunned his or her entire adult life. This person will most likely exhibit severe forms of some of the Fourth Born characteristics, such as anger and an inability to think for him- or herself. These traits will not be as pronounced in a Fourth Born who came from a home where older brothers and sisters loved the little guy to pieces, took him everywhere, and let him be a part of everything. The type of environment we were raised in, then, helps to make each one of us an individual and to differentiate us from others who share the same Birth Order.

The best way to determine your Birth Order Personality is to start with your own chronological birth order. As previously discussed, most of the time a person's psychological Birth Order position will be the same as his or her chronological birth order position.

We've already been through many of the exceptions to this general rule. A big one, of course, is when the family brings in someone to help after the second child is born and the first-born remains an Only Child as a result. You can flip back to the previous chapters to review some of those rules, but stick with us now. We have a pretty easy and fun way for you to pinpoint your Birth Order Personality.

Usually, the best way to determine if something fits is to

try it on. Since we can't design a removable Personality for you, we've tried to come up with the next best thing. How about a T-shirt?

The following pages will give you something to try on, at least in your mind. Each T-shirt represents a different Birth Order position through particular messages printed on it. As the experts in the fitting room, we can help you see which one looks best on you.

Just like shopping for clothes in the real world, it's often a good idea to have someone else along to give you an opinion. A spouse, a sibling, or a close friend might be able to provide you with some insights. The shirt you end up choosing should be the one that feels most comfortable to you and should help reveal your psychological Birth Order.

Each T-shirt has a statement on the front and another on the back. The statement on the back of the shirt reveals the thought behind the attitude expressed on the front. Together, they summarize each Birth Order position. The Birth Order descriptions that follow each T-shirt should help you keep things in context and thereby help you decide where you belong.

Only Child

The Only Child T-shirt says "Leave me alone" on the front and "I'd rather do it myself!" on the back. This is pretty much what the Only Child Personality will say to parents who give them more attention than they want.

If you pay attention to adult Onlies, you can see how they continue

to give out signals that they want to be left alone. They may talk constantly, for example, which is enough to make anyone want to leave them alone, or they may appear to be busy paying attention to someone or something else while someone is trying to talk to them.

An engineer named Larry learned how to do something about the problem he was having with his boss, once he realized the boss was a true Only Child. When Larry would go in to talk with him, his boss would shuffle papers, look out the window, or read his mail. This drove Larry crazy, as it would anyone else.

The supervisor was doing a good job of saying, "Leave me alone," without uttering a word. His behavior was posing problems for Larry and the other employees, however, who needed information from him in order to do their jobs.

Larry was smart enough to share this problem with someone who knew about Birth Order Personality. The next time his boss gave out some of his "leave me alone" signals, Larry quietly closed and locked the supervisor's office door, set his papers down on the desk, and sat down and took off his shoes.

At that point he had his boss's attention. Next, Larry climbed up on the man's desk and jumped up and down a few times. Then he got off, put his shoes back on, and, grinning, asked his boss, "Now will you listen to me?"

His boss got the message, grinned back, and listened like he had never listened before. After that, if the supervisor ever started shuffling papers, while Larry was trying to talk to him, he would ask, "Do I have to get up on your desk again?" His supervisor would smile and they would get on with business.

When Onlies are invited to do something they don't feel like doing, they often respond, "I don't know." In general, they often use the phrase "You know." By being noncommittal, it is their hope that you will not pursue the matter and will leave them alone.

Onlies tend to avoid situations in which they feel intruded upon, like having certain people at their homes. Their body language, excessive talking, apparent disinterest, and feeling that "I'd rather do it myself" all send the "Leave me alone" message expressed on the front of the shirt.

Is this you? Do you act or feel like this? Think about it. If the shirt fits, you are an Only Child.

First Born

The First Born T-shirt says "I don't know" on the front and "What do you think?" on the back. Like all the T-shirt messages, these statements also encompass unspoken gestures. Remember that the First Born has chosen approval, respect, and admiration over unconditional love, and, as a result, often loses track of what he or she thinks and feels.

First Borns often look to others to find out what to think and feel and, in many cases, do. The First Born will often nod when you are having a discussion with him or her so that you will keep talking. He or she will appear interested in what you have to say, as if you have his or her full attention.

The First Born often says "Uh-huh" or "Is that right?" to encourage you to keep going and offer more details. The First Born makes you want to keep on talking.

If you are thinking that you yourself might be a First Born, try a little experiment with someone who cares about you. Have a conversation with that person and ask him or her to write down the number of times you respond in the ways described above.

    See if you can try to respond differently in the future, although the seeking of approval is such a key element of the First Born's Birth Order Personality, and this might pose such a drastic physical and mental change that you may not be able to do it. Regardless of what happens, keep in mind that First Borns have lots to offer just as they are.

Second Born

The Second Born T-shirt reads "That won't work" on the front and "It's not good enough" on the back, because the Second Born child works on overcoming his or her feelings of inadequacy by finding fault with the First Born and by trying to keep from being outperformed by him or her.

    This kind of behavior happens all the time in families. If a First Born decides to do something nice by washing all the dishes, the Second Born will think of something to say like, "He used too much soap," or "The floor got all wet." This type of response can apply to about 592 things that happen during the course of a week.

    Second Borns really want to keep the First Born humble and use the statements on the T-shirt as a way of doing so. As adults, Second Borns continue this behavior in a variety of ways. If someone they work with comes up with a new idea or a new way of doing things, the Second Born will try and undermine them with a million questions: "Where would we find the time to do that?" "Are people going to want to do that?" "Have you considered what that would take?" "Have you really thought this through?"

Sometimes a Second Born will also say something like, "I've heard other people are not in favor of this," when this is just not the case. Saying so is just another way for the Second Born to keep another Birth Order from looking good.

Second Borns can often get their message across without saying a word. They may frown, offer a piercing look, rub the side of their face or their chin, tilt their head just a little bit, or maybe put their hands on their hips.

With their verbal and nonverbal means of communicating, Second Borns can get the rest of us to think of things from every angle. We had better be thinking, because they are. You can count on that.

Third Born

The Third Born T-shirt, which says "No Problem" on the front and "It doesn't bother me any" on the back, reflects the Third Born's efforts to try and protect him- or herself

from the Second Born, who is always trying to get a rise out of the Third Born.

It's very important for Third Borns to know that the rest of us believe that nothing bothers them. Third Borns who are going through a tough time may hide their problems under a smile. Watch out if you figure this out. Keep some tissues handy.

Third Borns actually end up making life difficult for themselves when they communicate the "no problem" feeling in words or gestures. Others quickly learn that they can take advantage of the Third Born—that if they ask it, the Third

Born will do it. Actually, it's not even always necessary to ask because the Third Born loves to volunteer.

Has a friend or someone you love ever said to you, "You have to learn how to say no"? That's something you would say to a Third Born. It's tough for Third Borns to decline a request for help or to let anyone know that some things really do get to them.

Third Borns say, "no problem" so often that it's a terrific way to identify them. Sometimes in therapy, Cliff Isaacson will ask someone whom he thinks is a Third Born to switch chairs, and the Third Born will almost always reply, "No problem."

These nice guys and gals of the world are easy to pick out. Just sit down and ask any of them if he or she could do something for you. The response will come quick and you will have identified a Third Born.

Fourth Born

The Fourth Born T-shirt says "Life isn't easy" on the front and "You have to try hard" on the back. Poor Fourth Borns feel frustrated from the day they're born, what else could they say?

This Birth Order keeps feeling rejected because they believe they are immature. As children, Fourth Borns felt that their older brothers and sisters never wanted them around and that that it was almost a miracle if they did anything right. That's why the Fourth Born child decided at a young age that it was necessary to "try hard."

Adult Fourth Borns perceive trying hard as a sign of being grown up and as having reached some level of maturity. Others, however, may see it as childish. It doesn't quite sit right when someone is constantly letting us know how tough they have it so they can prove how mature they are. Some other Fourth Borns go in the opposite direction. They could be walking on nails and never complain. Since they truly believe that life isn't supposed to be easy, why in the world would they complain about a little thing like bloody feet?

Fourth Borns communicate "life isn't easy" by saying just that and by using the words "I'm trying." They don't "do" things, they "try" to do things. They ask questions like "How am I supposed to do that?" or "What am I supposed to do when he says that?" They end up making life difficult for themselves by appearing puzzled and uncomprehending, accusing others of having it easy, and generally doing things the hard way.

• • • • •

There you have it, life on a shirt. Getting to understand these Birth Order messages and the ways in which they are expressed can enable someone to pick out another's Birth Order Personality quickly. When you become skilled at identifying a Birth Order Personality based on one of these messages, people will think you are a mind reader. You will have opened the door to understanding, which is the key to the world.

Are you ready for some new information now that you have mastered all of this? Birth Order can be a very helpful tool in a marriage—keep reading if you want to see how.

Even the most powerful human being has
a limited sphere of strength. Draw him
outside of that sphere and into your own
and his strength will dissipate.
—Morihei Ueshiba

Chapter Twelve

I Do . . . Well, Sort Of: Birth Order Personality and Marriage

By now you should have a basic understanding of how Birth
Order Personality works in our lives. Knowing how your own
Birth Order Personality affects what you do and how you do
it provides a foundation for understanding the ways in which
your Personality influences your choice of marriage partner.

The true romantic might be throwing in the towel at this
point. "What about love at first sight?" he or she may be
asking. "What about passion and romance and just falling in
love gracefully without worrying about all this stuff?"

If you are married or in love or falling in love or looking
for love, you need to keep reading! Birth Order Personality
offers you a chance to enhance what you already have. Don't
you feel better when you understand why your spouse acts
in a certain way? Of course you do.

But before we begin, there is one point that begs clarification. In order to assess most clearly the effects of Birth Order on relationships, we will focus on marriage rather trying to apply Birth Order to all romantic relationships. For those contemplating marriage, this chapter may help you anticipate what you will experience. If you are living together, you may decide that your relationship is good the way it is without marriage. On the other hand, knowing what Birth Order effects you can anticipate might make marriage more desirable.

The fact is that you are more compatible with some people than with others, based on the way your Birth Order Personalities interact. Looking back, you may be able to recognize that this was the case in your own family growing up, while you were in school, and, later, when you entered the exciting—and sometimes cold and cruel—world of dating.

Birth Order can help you to better understand why you are attracted to some people but not to others. Perhaps in the past you have tried to force relationships. You want to like him or her, but something just doesn't feel right between the two of you. Some people force their feelings to the point where they actually marry or enter a long-term relationship with someone who is not right for them and end up creating more than a few disasters.

It's also true, of course, that many other factors besides Birth Order affect a marriage. Differences in age, cultural background, education, and values can all make or break a relationship. A couple's health, financial condition, parenting styles, relationships with in-laws, and intellectual compatibility can also deeply impact a love match.

With all of that in mind, it's important to know that your marriage may not fit the particular descriptions of Birth Order relationships. We may suggest that someone of your Birth Order should never marry someone of another particular Birth Order, and you may have already done so and are wildly happy. That's where individual qualities, experiences, and circumstances come into play. Remember, Birth Order is not meant to put everyone into a little box. We are who we are. Got that? It's pretty important.

If the following information does not seem to fit your particular circumstances, there may still be some pieces of knowledge there that you can store away and use at some point. One woman who was reading through the Marriage Compatibility Chart jumped for joy when she read that Second Borns often fall in love at first sight with an Only Child Birth Order Personality. This is exactly what had happened with this woman. She had fallen in love with her future husband in less than ten minutes after she'd first met him, married him in just a few months, and has since had fourteen wonderful years of married life with him. After she read the chart, she quickly phoned her husband at work and said, "Honey, we are a match made in heaven." Her husband laughed, fell in love with her all over again, and picked up some flowers on the way home. You just never know how and when Birth Order might affect you.

It is important to know that Birth Order impacts a marriage most powerfully when one or both partners come from traumatic backgrounds. This is true, as we have mentioned, with Birth Order in general. In unhappy homes, Birth Order traits become stronger as children learn how to cope. These traits, which keep some of us in rigid lines, can cause problems in a marriage.

Obviously, couples in which both partners have come from happy homes have the best prospect for a happy marriage. If they had good role models and knew they were loved, their marriage may escape the negative effects of Birth Order since they can become flexible in relating to each other.

The emotional outbursts of the Only Child, the ultimatums of the First Born, the criticisms of the Second Born, the verbal attacks of the Third Born, and the pushiness of the Fourth Born can all be avoided. On the other hand, those who have grown up in dysfunctional homes have developed strong Birth Order characteristics, which are the cause of adversarial behavior.

The following Marriage Compatibility Chart should be used only after you have identified your Birth Order. You may have a successful marriage that the chart says does not work, and if so, bravo! You are a well-adjusted, happy person who has been able to make positive changes in your life.

As you will see, the chart uses your own Birth Order as well as that of a same-sex parent to determine your perfect match. Why does the Birth Order of the parent of the same sex matter? Doesn't a woman look for a guy like her father, and doesn't a man look for a woman like his mother? This sounds logical but it is incorrect. A girl, without realizing it, looks for a man like her mother. This is because every love relationship begins as companionship, and she had companionship, whether good, bad, or indifferent, with her mother, so she's naturally going to be drawn to someone with whom she can have similar companionship. A man, likewise, had companionship with his father, so he is naturally drawn to women with whom he can have that kind of companionship. Therefore, the marital relationship tends to be a repeat of the childhood relationship with the parent of the same sex.

With a perfect Birth Order match, as outlined in the following chart, the marriage tends to be the most stable. Of course, psychotherapy for the relationship may be in order if the relationship with the parent of the opposite sex was bad.

Unfortunately, there is no perfect match for the First Born with a First, Second, or Third Born parent of the same sex. This does not mean that First Borns cannot be happily married. It simply means that more attention must be given to

developing the relationship, maintaining it, and getting help
when needed.

Few marriages are a perfect match according to Birth
Order. Nevertheless, they can be happy marriages. Blame
your problems on Birth Order, not each other, and do what
you can to have a happy marriage.

Now, let's take a look at the chart and then get into
some more specifics about how Birth Order can influence
marriage relationships.

Birth Order Marriage Compatibility Chart For Women

Birth Order	Mother	Perfect Match
Only Child	Only Child	Only Child with Only Child Father
Only Child	First Born	First Born with Only Child or Fourth Born Father
Only Child	Second Born	Second Born with Only Child or Fourth Born Father
Only Child	Third Born	Third Born with Only Child or Fourth Born Father
Only Child	Fourth Born	Fourth Born with Only Child or Fourth Born Father
First Born	Only Child	Only Child with First Born Father
First Born	First Born	None
First Born	Second Born	None
First Born	Third Born	None
First Born	Fourth Born	Only Child with First Born Father
Second Born	Only Child	Only Child with Second Born Father
Second Born	First Born	Second Born with First Born Father
Second Born	Second Born	Third Born with First Born Father
Second Born	Third Born	Fourth Born with First Born Father
Second Born	Fourth Born	Only Child with Second Born Father

(continued)

Birth Order Marriage Compatibility Chart For Women (continued)

Birth Order	Mother	Perfect Match
Third Born	Only Child	Only Child with Third Born Father
Third Born	First Born	Second Born with Second Born Father
Third Born	Second Born	Third Born with Second Born Father
Third Born	Third Born	Fourth Born with Second Born Father
Third Born	Fourth Born	Only Child with Third Born Father
Fourth Born	Only Child	Only Child with Fourth Born Father
Fourth Born	First Born	Second Born with Third Born Father
Fourth Born	Second Born	Third Born with Third Born Father
Fourth Born	Third Born	Fourth Born with Third Born Father
Fourth Born	Fourth Born	Only Child with Fourth Born Father

For Men

Birth Order	Father	Perfect Match
Only Child	Only Child	Only Child with Only Child Mother
Only Child	First Born	First Born with Only Child or Fourth Born Mother
Only Child	Second Born	Second Born with Only Child or Fourth Born Mother
Only Child	Third Born	Third Born with Only Child or Fourth Born Mother
Only Child	Fourth Born	Fourth Born with Only Child or Fourth Born Mother
First Born	Only Child	Only Child with First Born Mother
First Born	First Born	None
First Born	Second Born	None
First Born	Third Born	None
First Born	Fourth Born	Only Child with First Born Mother
Second Born	Only Child	Only Child with Second Born Mother
Second Born	First Born	Second Born with First Born Mother
Second Born	Second Born	Third Born with First Born Mother
Second Born	Third Born	Fourth Born with First Born Mother
Second Born	Fourth Born	Only Child with Second Born Mother

(continued)

Birth Order Marriage Compatibility Chart For Men *(continued)*

Birth Order	Mother	Perfect Match
Third Born	Only Child	Only Child with Third Born Mother
Third Born	First Born	Second Born with Second Born Mother
Third Born	Second Born	Third Born with Second Born Mother
Third Born	Third Born	Fourth Born with Second Born Mother
Third Born	Fourth Born	Only Child with Third Born Mother
Fourth Born	Only Child	Only Child with Fourth Born Mother
Fourth Born	First Born	Second Born with Third Born Mother
Fourth Born	Second Born	Third Born with Third Born Mother
Fourth Born	Third Born	Fourth Born with Third Born Mother
Fourth Born	Fourth Born	Only Child with Fourth Born Mother

These matches are "perfect" in the sense that they are the easiest marriages to make work, barring other factors. They contain a natural compatibility factor. Any marriage can work, and work well; however, some require more learning from the partners, more adjustment to each other.

The most ideal marriages are made when a man chooses a woman according to the secondary Birth Order characteristics he inherited from his father, and a woman chooses a man according to the secondary Birth Order characteristics she inherited from her mother. When this happens, the couple will be compatible in terms of Birth Order. The marriage will be a comfortable one, and the couple should enjoy smooth sailing. This may sound complicated, but we will try and keep it simple, as being married is hard enough, no matter how well adjusted and wonderful we all are.

It should be kept in mind that married couples may relate to each other in many ways that are not Birth Order related. One example of this is a couple that finally discovered that the relationships they had with their parents while growing up, rather than their Birth Order Personalities, were playing a crucial role in their marriage. This couple was violent with each other on a regular basis. She would hit him. He would hit her. When a counselor asked them about their relationships with their parents of the same sex, they came up with some interesting answers.

The man grew up angry with his father and wishing that he could hit him, and the woman had experienced the same type of feelings about her mother. They were subconsciously fulfilling their wishes by hitting each other. Ouch. Makes sense when you think about it, but their behavior in married life was tied to things that happened to them as children that had nothing at all to do with their Birth Order.

Another example would be the woman who, as a child, was expected to take care of her mother. As a little girl, this woman had had to do everything from the cooking and cleaning to making phone calls for her mother. Guess what? This woman ended up marrying a man who needed taking care of, just as her mother had. Birth Order did not have much to do with her choice of a spouse.

Family relationships not related to Birth Order can also have a positive effect on marriages. A woman who had a great relationship with her own mother can expect to have the same kind of relationship with her husband. By the same token, if a man had a loving relationship with his father, he should have a beautiful marriage. Yet, if one spouse comes into the marriage having had a good relationship with the same-sex parent, and the other comes in having had a bad relationship, there can be problems. The couple may need to seek some professional help in order to learn how to be happy together.

Birth Order alone, then, cannot predict what the quality or durability of a good marriage will be. Birth Order can give you some guidelines, offer some suggestions, and show you what could be happening because of Birth Order Personality. If there is a problem, Birth Order can sometimes help you discover the reasons why.

The following Marriage Relationship Guide has been designed with the idea that the child and the parent are of the same sex. Remember, this is only a guide and it may not apply specifically to your situation, but there may be something you can take away with you.

Marriage Relationship Guide

Only Child with an Only Child Parent: Best choice of spouse is Only Child. They live in separate worlds together. This Only Child will be frustrated with a First, Third, or Fourth Born spouse, in trying get them organized or emotionally reacting to their lack of order. He or she gets along better with a Second Born, but dislikes the Second Born's correcting.

Only Child with a First Born Parent: Best choice of spouse is First Born. Tends to organize own world, gets frustrated trying to discover what spouse wants. Tends to feel pressured with Second, Third, and Fourth Borns, but not with another Only Child.

Only Child with a Second Born Parent: Best choice of spouse is a Second Born. Is comfortable with the reliability of the Second Born. With all other Birth Orders, except an Only Child, would feel frustrated with lack of order. With another Only Child would feel isolated.

Only Child with a Third Born Parent: Best choice of spouse is a Third Born. Might react negatively to Third Born chaotic behavior but feels free to express emotions with this Birth Order Personality. With a First or Fourth Born spouse, this person may feel controlled. With a Second Born or another Only Child, he or she might feel unstimulated and bored.

Only Child with a Fourth Born Parent: Best choice of spouse is a Fourth Born. Unfortunately, this is most likely going to be a difficult relationship if he or she were in conflict with the parent during childhood. May feel the pressure to care for the spouse. Would tend to overreact to natural foibles of a spouse of another Birth Order.

First Born with an Only Child Parent: Best choice of spouse is an Only Child. Would allow the spouse to organize things. Is unlikely to marry a First Born. Might find a Second Born compatible but intimidating. Would expect a Third or Fourth Born spouse to be more orderly than he or she can be.

First Born with a First Born Parent: Best choice of spouse is a Second Born. This marital combination is rare, because a Second Born would not find the First Born to be the best choice. This First Born would tend to be passive in any marital relationship.

First Born with a Second Born Parent: Best choice of spouse is a Third Born. This First Born tends to marry the fearful-type Third Born. A Third Born, however, would not find the First Born to be the best choice. This marriage would require more than average maintenance.

First Born with a Third Born Parent: Best choice of spouse is a Fourth Born. Married to a Fourth Born, the First Born tends to feel comfortable. A Fourth Born, however, would not find the First Born to be the best choice. With other Birth Order spouses, this First Born tends to feel powerless.

First Born with a Fourth Born Parent: Best choice of spouse is an Only Child. Tends to feel comfortable with an Only Child, respecting that person's freedom. With other Birth Order spouses would tend to be wary, defensive.

Second Born with an Only Child Parent: Best choice of spouse is an Only Child. This relationship can begin with love at first sight. This Second Born would tend to feel critical of a First, Third, and Fourth Born spouse for being disorganized. He or she might feel a lack of emotion with another Second Born.

Second Born with a First Born Parent: Best choice of spouse is a Second Born. Would expect partner to be perfectionist. Would tend to feel irritated with another Birth Order, except possibly with the Only Child.

Second Born with a Second Born Parent: Best choice of spouse is a Third Born. Would be drawn to the fearless-type Third Born, expecting him or her to be strong. Would tend to be critical of the weaknesses of other Birth Orders.

Second Born with Third Born Parent: Best choice of spouse is a Fourth Born. Would tend to capitulate to the Fourth Born in decision-making. With other Birth Orders would tend to be agreeable.

Second Born with a Fourth Born Parent: Best choice of spouse is an Only Child. Tends to be a good relationship. With other Birth Orders, this Second Born would tend to go along with the spouse's desires.

Third Born with an Only Child Parent: Best choice of spouse is an Only Child. Tends to be a good relationship on an emotional level. Tends to be disappointed with other Birth Orders because of inability to connect emotionally.

Third Born with a First Born Parent: Best choice of spouse is a Second Born. Tends to have the upper hand in this relationship. May be adversarial with a spouse of another Birth Order.

Third Born with a Second Born Parent: Best choice of spouse is a Third Born. This tends to be a harmonious relationship, with one being a fearless-type Third Born and the other a fearful type. Tends to be easy to get along with in marriage with other Birth Orders.

Third Born with a Third Born Parent: Best choice of spouse is a Fourth Born. The Fourth Born would tend to have the upper hand emotionally. Would expect another Birth Order spouse to be strong.

Third Born with a Fourth Born Parent: Best choice of spouse is an Only Child. Tends to connect emotionally with the Only Child. With other Birth Orders is apt to feel defensive.

Fourth Born with an Only Child Parent: Best choice of spouse is an Only Child. The Fourth Born, however, tends to be pushy in the relationship. With other Birth Orders this Fourth Born may feel overpowered.

Fourth Born with a First Born Parent: Best choice of spouse is a Second Born. The Fourth Born tends to have his or her way in this relationship. With other Birth Orders this Fourth Born tends to be passive.

Fourth Born with a Second Born Parent: Best choice of spouse is a Third Born. The Fourth Born tends to have the upper hand in this relationship. He or she expects to be able to manipulate those of all Birth Orders.

Fourth Born with a Third Born Parent: Best choice of spouse is a Fourth Born. Compatible, but without a power structure; tends to stop communicating under stress. Tends to clam up where there is conflict with all Birth Order spouses.

Fourth Born with a Fourth Born Parent: Best choice of spouse is an Only Child. Tends to be frustrated with not being able to be close in this relationship. Tends to feel left out by spouses of other Birth Orders.

This list is suggestive rather than definitive. So many variables go into making up a relationship that they cannot be fully defined. This guide may explain why a particular relationship is the way it is, but it will not explain all relationships.

Choosing the "best" in terms of Birth Order, of course, does not guarantee happiness. There are other factors involved. However, the best marriage choice is the easiest person with whom to relate in a marriage. The best choice is the one with whom a person is most likely to be comfortable over the long haul.

Let's give you a few examples of how Birth Order Personality can work in a marriage. These are pretty specific and, once again, may not pertain to you. But this is still a great way to learn about the dynamics of Birth Order Personalities.

As you know from the preceding charts, Second Born and Only Child Personalities are drawn to each other. Sue, for example, an Only Child Birth Order Personality, likes to organize and was first drawn to her Second Born husband, Bob, because of his dependability. Although Bob doesn't make many promises, he does keep the ones he makes. This is especially true when it comes to being on time. Bob is always there when he says he is going to be there and is often a bit early. Sue liked the fact that she could count on him and that he'd do what he said he'd do.

If you add these traits to Bob's sense of loyalty, it's a cinch that Sue soon felt secure with him. Since Bob is more logical than emotional, he did not smother Sue, which felt pretty good to her. As an Only Child she hates to be smothered. It didn't take Sue long to fall in love with Bob the Second Born.

Sue is quite a talker. She loves to tell the whole story in very specific detail. Because Bob is a perfectionist he wants to know the details and liked that Sue would share with him. Because Sue seemed tuned into his feelings, Bob felt like she cared about him. Second Borns would rather pull out each one of their hairs with tweezers than think that someone does not care about them. Even though Bob keeps a tight rein on his own emotions, he was happy that Sue was able to share hers with him.

Onlies and Seconds are a very common combination in Birth Order. These Birth Orders may fall in love at first sight, second sight, or third sight; in any case, the falling in love happens pretty darn fast. Yet although Onlies and Seconds may start out as perfect couples, their relationships are not necessarily problem-free.

With Sue and Bob, a bit of friction developed after they had been married awhile. Bob began trying to pass on his perfectionism to his wife by correcting the things she did. If she made a great dinner, for example, he would never tell her that. Instead, he might say something like, "The peas would taste a bit better if you made a nice white sauce to go along with them." Poor Sue. She began to feel terrible. She hates being corrected and she discovered that she was living with Mr. Perfect.

Sue began reacting to Bob's suggestions in anger. Bob, unable to understand what she was so angry about, was hurt. In his heart of hearts, he thought he was just trying to help Sue and had no clue that his helpful suggestions were upsetting her. They began to argue, but not enough to break up the marriage. Pretty soon, Bob stopped giving Sue suggestions for improving—but he never replaced the suggestions with anything else. Instead of saying, "Great dinner, sweetie," Bob would say nothing at all, and this once-happy couple ended up with almost no emotional connection.

When a few babies came along, Bob and Sue became distracted and never took a second to think about their emotional estrangement until the children were grown and they were alone again. At that point, they began to realize that they lacked the emotional bond necessary for a happy relationship.

Imagine now how things might have turned out if Bob had known what to say to his wife. If they had both understood Birth Order Personality and its implications for relationships, this could have been a much happier and more fulfilled match. Let's hope Bob and Sue buy *The Birth Order Effect* and are able to rekindle their old flame.

The most difficult marriage that you will find is when a Fourth Born marries an Only Child woman. Before marriage, their relationship appears to have been made in heaven. The Fourth Born man treats the Only Child like a queen, and she loves every minute of his attention. The man comes across as unselfish, attentive, giving, and accepting. This woman cannot believe her luck in finding this gem of a man. He, in turn, is attracted to her because she is responsive, expressive, and always considers his feelings. They get along perfectly until their marriage vows are spoken. Then life as they know it is over.

This Fourth Born is driven by the thought that all good things must come to an end, so he ends up bringing the fun-filled days and nights they experienced during their courtship to an end. When his new wife makes it clear that she wants things to go on the way they had been, the husband gets angry with her. As an Only Child, she wants to do things right, and so she works at trying to keep things the way they were, while her husband works at ending the good parts of the relationship. Neither has a clue as to why they no longer seem to get along. Each one blames the other. In many cases, this cycle will only end with the breakup of the couple.

A common type of marriage involves the fearful-type Third Born woman who seeks emotional security with a man who is no emotional threat to her, and the First Born male who is out of touch with himself and who appears nonassertive, compliant, and completely harmless. Joe and Amy was such a couple. They had been married for twenty-one years when he finally decided he had had enough of his wife's overdependence on him and her tendency to play the perfect victim while blaming everything on him. He got involved with another woman and expected that this would end the marriage, but his wife forgave him. He later got involved with someone else, yet still the marriage stayed intact.

No matter what Joe did his wife forgave him. He finally filed for divorce, quit his job, and moved away. After Joe left her, Amy was finally able to find herself and began to live as an independent, self-fulfilled woman.

Knowledge and understanding of Birth Order Personality can help a marriage to grow and change and blossom. It can lead to insights and behaviors that may be as simple as saying the right words, really listening to what your spouse has to say, or making certain you know exactly how your spouse feels, but that have the potential to preserve and enhance a marriage.

The power of Birth Order Personality is immense. If you think it has some strong effects on your love life, wait 'till you see what knowing about Birth Order Personality can do for your parenting skills. You may just earn the Mother or Father of the Year award if you can make it through the next chapter.

Chapter Thirteen

He's Definitely Your Son: Birth Order and Parenting

Feeling brave? Go outside and stop the average looking man or woman on the street. Ask this simple question and see what kind of answer you get: "What's the hardest thing you have ever done?"

Anyone who is a mother or father will most likely say, "Being a parent." Although raising children is the most wonderful thing in the world, it's definitely an occupation that is more than challenging. The manner in which one approaches this mostly joyful task is significantly influenced by Birth Order Personality.

In these modern days of constant change, parenting has taken on new sets of challenges and obstacles that need more than a "how-to" handbook or some advice from Grandma and Grandpa. It's no longer enough to prepare our sons and daughters for life in the fields, factories, or college.

Imagine a family dinner conversation circa 1953: "How about those Cardinals?" "Do you think it will rain tomorrow?" or "Grandma baked us an apple pie for dinner!" Compare their exchange with the type of conversation that might be heard around today's family dinner table: "Daddy, what's pre-marital sex?" "Why are drugs bad?" and "Did you hear about the kid who brought a gun to our school?"

Life and the skills necessary to be a positive and effective parent have definitely changed. Children today are dealing with issues on the grade-school playground that we may not have confronted until college. It's not easy, but no one ever said parenthood was a constant picnic.

Since parents bring their own individual Birth Order Personality into their relationships with their children, it would make sense that children do the same thing with their parents. A wise parent would not treat a First Born, say, the same way he or she treats a Third Born

Out of all the areas in which Birth Order can affect your life, it can bring the most positive results to parenting. Wouldn't understanding and respecting the fact that your Only Child son or daughter loves to be alone and hates to be bothered, for example, be preferable to trying to force after-school play dates down his or her throat every other day? How about the son who gets angry if you go into his room and move the books he has lined up on his bed? Instead of wondering why he's so compulsive, now you'll understand that he's just behaving like a Second Born.

Life as a parent can be as simple or as complicated as you make it. Of course, it can be difficult and challenging at times, but it certainly doesn't have to be round-the-clock torture. Parenting takes on a whole new meaning and flavor when Birth Order is understood and acknowledged.

Whether or not they know about Birth Order Personality, individuals parent according to their own Birth Order

Personality and that of their children. Is there one child who likes to be in charge? Another who loves to sit alone and not be bothered? Another one who is always ready to jump off the nearest cliff?

Every human being in the world has his or her own Birth Order Personality, and parents can save themselves a world of hurt if they pay attention to the individual Personalities of their children. Before we plunge into this exciting realm of life, we should mention a few general parental Birth Order observations that can help you to better understand how this all works.

While gender does not seem to play a role in Birth Order development, children do appear to relate to parents according to gender. Children usually take the parent of the same gender as a role model and the parent of the opposite gender as a director. In other words, a child will watch the parent of the same sex and listen to the parent of the opposite sex. For example, a daughter will learn how to act from watching every thing her mother does. This same daughter will listen closely to what her dad tells her: "Daddy says I can be or do anything in the whole world," she might say. "I believe him because he's my daddy."

Thus, children will pattern their behavior after the parent of the same gender and develop their self-concepts according to the feedback from the parent of the opposite gender. One thirteen-year-old boy, for example, started putting on aftershave and wearing a sweatshirt every day, just like his father did, but he listened to what his mother told him about being sensitive and aware of how his actions affected others at school.

If you think about this for a minute, some personal example may pop into your mind. One mother was amazed when her little girl told her one evening that she was going to start washing her own hair, picking out her clothes, and taking care of all her personal hygiene. "Mom, you showed me how, so now I can do it," the little girl explained. The mother did not remember doing anything other than talking to her daughter as she gave her a bath or explaining how you put the shampoo on first and then the conditioner.

That's exactly how this works. This same daughter trusted every single thing her father told her. She listened to him, always paid attention to what he said, and believed in herself because her father had given her a healthy self-image.

As young children, we all needed role models to show us how to be adults. A boy needs to look up to a man (or men) to learn what it is to be a man. A girl needs to look up to a woman (or women) to learn what it is to be a woman. In single parent families, a child usually fulfills the need for a role model through some other adult with whom he or she has a lot of contact. This person could be an uncle or aunt, a teacher, or even someone at church—anyone the child is spending lots of time with.

This might be a good time to take a look back at your own Birth Order chapter to refresh your memory and see your traits and characteristics laid out right in front of you. Don't be scared. Keep in mind that your kids love you and look up to you and are learning how to behave and act for the rest of their lives because of all the great things you do everyday.

Once you are ready, you can move ahead to the following charts, which will help you to put the challenges of parenting into some neat Birth Order Personality explanations. As you read through these charts, it's important to remember that parenting styles can be influenced or modified by another parent in the family or, if you are a single parent, by a significant other or another adult your child spends a lot of time with.

Also, remember that since each of us is unique, you may not see all of these parenting characteristics in yourself.

Birth Order Parenting Styles

Only Child Parent: Is largely concerned about being fair with the children, which means treating them all alike. This parent deals with problems by organizing space or time. This parent expresses love toward children by giving them space and time. May try to leave the other parent out of parenting decisions.

Potential Problems: Children may fight with each other over what is fair.

First Born Parent: Tends to exercise power and is concerned about obedience. Deals with problems by demanding respect from children in terms of instant obedience; issues ultimatums when children are disobedient. Either expects agreement from the partner or abdicates to the partner. Expresses love by giving permission to the children.

Potential Problems: Rebellion in the children, especially in a fearless-type Third Born child.

Second Born Parent: Tends to rely on authority, laying down rules. Deals with problems by laying out consequences. Expects support from the other parent. If that parent is a Fourth Born, will tend to make the rules to fit what the Fourth Born wants. Expresses love by giving correction to help the children toward perfection.

Potential Problems: Children experience depression, especially a Second Born child.

Third Born Parent: Tends to rely on persuasion, using reason to deal with the children. Deals with problems by expressing disappointment, possibly giving children the silent treatment. May get into conflict with the other parent if he or she tries to use power, authority, or force over the children. Expresses love by seeking to please the children.

Potential Problems: Children become unruly.

Fourth Born Parent: Tends to use force to deal with children, or is passive. Deals with problems by punishing the children or by getting angry with the other parent for the children's behavior. Expresses love by giving things to the children.

Potential Problems: May favor one child over the others; may make a scapegoat out of one.

Did you find yourself in there? Most people do. This should give you a good idea of your parenting style and what signs and scents your children are picking up from you.

Now that you understand your own parenting style a bit better, let's see how the children react to all of this. We already know that children have unique ways of challenging parents based on their Birth Order Personality. Some of us may experience this more than others, depending on how strong the Birth Order Personality of our child happens to be.

In attending the needs and wants of children according to their particular Birth Order, this chart can help you tremendously. You may want to keep it somewhere where you can refer to it frequently.

Needs of Children According to Birth Order

Only Child: Needs time and space with freedom to do what he or she wants. Responds to statements such as, "I don't know about you, but . . . " (to get the child to listen); "You deserve to have . . . " (to get the child to feel loved); and "You can be angry if you want but . . . " (as confrontation). Gets along best with an Only Child parent, experiencing more difficulty with each Birth Order, with the Fourth Born parent being the most difficult.

First Born: Needs to experience unconditional love. Responds to statements such as, "You might not agree with this, but . . . " (to get the child to listen); "You did well, but I love you because you're you" (to make the child feel loved); and "I would appreciate if you would . . . " (to confront the child). Tends to try to overpower parents as he or she gets older. *Yes!*

Second Born: Needs to experience acceptance. Responds to statements such as, "This is not perfect but . . . " (to get the child to listen); "That's all right. I love you anyway," (to make the child feel loved after he or she has put self down); and "You know in your heart who's going to lose if you do that" (to confront the child). Is especially affectionate at elementary school age, but can develop oppositional defiance disorder in teens.

Third Born: Needs to feel safe. Responds to statements such as, "Please . . . " (because they appeal to the Third Born's desire to please and therefore produce a positive response); "I'm sorry you're having to go through that . . . " (to make the child feel loved); and "I'm disappointed you did that . . . " (to confront the child). The fearless-type Third Born may be a danger to him or herself, but the fearful type is reluctant to leave the safety of home to do things.

Fourth Born: Needs to be included. Responds to statements such as, "It may be hard for you to believe, but . . . " (to get the child to listen); "You are part of this family" (to make the child feel loved); and "Stop it! Do this . . . " (to confront the child). The Fourth Born child may fade into the woodwork unless parents take pains to include him or her.

Talk about words to live by. Haven't you ever wondered what to say to your children to get them motivated? How about something wise to let them know you understand who they are and what they want to be? What about saying something forceful to let them know you mean business but that you still care about them? The charts can help you get to those places with your children. There really are some perfect things to say and some perfect ways to act around each one of your little darlings.

As those of us who have children know, parenting really does offer a bit of the good, the bad, the ugly, the wonderful, the challenging, the beautiful, the frustrating, and just about every other adjective you can think of. By knowing how each one of your children is affected by his or her own Birth Order Personality, you can help them to grow and mature in ways that can make parenting more joy than pain. Really. It does work.

Knowing and understanding Birth Order can't help but make life easier and simpler for you. Here's an example of a mother who could've changed her life and the life of her daughter had she known about Birth Order. The mother was a Second Born married to a Fourth Born. This couple had two daughters, a First Born and a Second Born. The Second Born daughter was giving her parents some trouble, so the mother sent her in for counseling. The counselor quickly discovered that the father was harassing this girl and that the mother constantly took the father's side. This made life difficult for the girl and caused her to start acting up in an effort to get her mother's attention, get some help, and get her dad off her back. The acting up, however, just made the situation worse.

It is very common for a Second Born mother to cater to a Fourth Born husband over the children. The natural inclination of the Second Born is to be a peacemaker and the pressure is on even more if one's spouse happens to be an angry Fourth Born.

In this case, the Second Born daughter was also a peacemaker who wanted to solve the problem of her father's poor treatment of her without causing disruption in the family. Consequently, she acted up rather than talking about the problem because she knew that her mother would take the side of her father anyway.

Imagine how much better this situation could've been handled if the mother had understood her own Birth Order as well as those of her husband and daughter: life could have been easier for all of them.

There are thousands and thousands of family situations that would benefit from an understanding of Birth Order. Birth Order can help with something as simple as getting a child to clean up her room or as complex as keeping a child from becoming alienated from his family for the rest of his life. Consider the following example.

Although there are many families where a Fourth Born parent and an Only Child are in harmony with each other, in one particular family there was a severe conflict between the Fourth Born mother and the Only Child daughter that could not be reconciled.

By the time the daughter graduated from high school, she and her mother had become so alienated from each other that the girl was not even welcome in the home most of the time. This alienation did not stem from the fact that the daughter was incorrigible or the mother evil, but because their Birth Order differences were not understood.

This girl just did not act like the mother would have acted in similar situations and the mother took offense at that. This type of conflict can occur between the parent and child of any Birth Order, but in this case is more pronounced because a Fourth Born parent's inclination is to use force to bring about conformity in a child.

Some of us may have been treated in this way ourselves or may have had friends who were embarrassed to have us visit them at their home because one or both of the parents criticized every single thing about them. Think back and you may remember a childhood friend whose parent humiliated them about something inconsequential in your presence.

Onlies, a tough-minded Birth Order Personality, do tend to turn out okay even under dire circumstances—as they are able to retreat into their own world when confronted with harsh treatment.

It isn't fair or correct, of course, to say that every Fourth Born parent will mistreat his or her children. Our own childhood, the behavior of another parent, and the desire in our own hearts and minds can also shape who we are and what kind of parent we are going to be.

On the positive side of this Fourth Born parenting coin is one father who, with his Third Born wife, provided an excellent, harmonious home for their children. This Fourth Born was a super-responsible father and husband who was able to nurture his children and provide boundaries for them. He was a terrific companion for his children and loved to spend time with them.

The desire to be a good parent can also overcome one's own negative childhood experience. One Only Child son who grew up with an abusive and alcoholic father decided from the time he was a young man that nothing was going to keep him from being a wonderful, supportive husband and father. Despite the fact that this young man could not remember his father ever telling him that he loved him, he learned how to be a loving father on his own.

Another dad decided to use what he had learned about Birth Order to get his Third Born to make a change. His daughter was a pretty typical—read "messy"—teenager. In fact, you could barely see the floor in her room. One day the father asked this Third Born daughter to clean up her room. He knew she wouldn't do it, and he was right. When he came home from work that evening, the room still looked like a disaster site. He told her that he was really disappointed that she had not cleaned up the room.

This Third Born daughter didn't like hearing that. She hated to disappoint her parents—or anyone for that matter. The next morning she set her alarm for 5 A.M. and went to town on her room. She threw things out, straightened up, and dusted her furniture. By the time her dad got up, her room was spotless. She went downstairs to ask him to come up to her room for a minute.

"Dad, are you still disappointed in me?" she asked him, beaming, as she showed him the results of her efforts. Of course he was not disappointed; he was beaming, too. His Birth Order–based intervention had worked; he had known that his Third Born daughter would not want to disappoint someone she cared about.

Birth Order Personality does not guarantee a clean and easy time of parenting. No one can offer you that. But again, understanding how your children think and feel and what motivates them can give you more than a leg up in these tough times of parenting.

You might want to try a simple experiment once you understand how this works. The father who got his Third Born daughter to clean her room probably felt as if he had won the lottery—and who can blame him? Motivate one of your own children to get a paper done early, mow the lawn, solve a conflict at school, or to get along better at home, and you will also feel as if you rule the world.

This new level of understanding will also bring you closer to your children. How could it not? Knowing what frustrates or upsets your children and what you can say to make them feel better will benefit both of you.

Birth Order Personality can help you to become a better parent, but every challenge that parenting offers will be unique. Be kind. Be gentle. Be firm. Act wisely. Laugh constantly. Love always—and just before you are ready to jump off the roof, get out *The Birth Order Effect* and reread this chapter. You will see yourself and your child in a new light.

> Don't be afraid to take one large
> step because you can't cross a
> chasm in two small leaps.
> —Lloyd George

Chapter Fourteen

"I Think I Can, I Think I Can": Getting over the Hill and Putting It All Together

Congratulations. If you have made it this far, you are a lot smarter and maybe even more fun to be around than you were before you started reading *The Birth Order Effect.* This will be especially true if you have been a good student—maybe taken a few notes, called in a few of your personal advisers, and tossed and turned a few times at night thinking about your own Birth Order Personality. Now we're going to tell you to lighten up. This is supposed to be fun and engaging. Well, okay, it's pretty serious stuff also, but you should be able to enjoy learning about yourself and the people around you.

If you're still having a hard time, call up a few of your pals and meet at the local restaurant for dinner. Consider trying to identify your friends' Birth Order Personalities during dinner as part of your final exam. Do you think you can identify individual Birth Order Personalities based on the interaction at the table? Of course you can; here's where the fun comes in.

Pay attention to see if your friends use any of the following types of phrases, which will help to give away their Birth Order Personalities.

> **Only Child:** "That was the best meal."
> **First Born:** "I think that was a good meal."
> **Second Born:** "That meal could have used more seasoning."
> **Third Born:** "You would love that meal."
> **Fourth Born:** "They could have done better."

Sometimes, just listening and watching will help you to determine a person's Birth Order Personality. This is pretty easy; it's also fun. Admit it.

Lest you believe that we are advocating that you think only in terms of Birth Order Personality, please be assured that we present it as just one way of looking at someone and of trying to understand relationships and behavior.

As you get to know these new Birth Order Personality concepts, they will gradually become second nature to you. You may be having a casual conversation with someone, chatting away about work, life, the stock market, when suddenly that person will say something that is so First Born. Will this change the nature of the conversation? Maybe or maybe not. But if the First Born begins to tell you about a problem or a concern they are dealing with, you could use what you know about Birth Order Personality to help him or her. Or you could just carry on with the inner knowledge that you now understand this person just a bit more than you did twenty minutes ago.

The different ways in which Birth Order Personality affects all of us will gradually begin to become more familiar to you, until you get to the point where it is fairly easy to define various aspects of your own Personality and those of the people with whom you deal on a daily basis.

This chapter will deal with some miscellaneous aspects of Birth Order Personality. Take sense of humor, for example. Each Personality has its own specific brand. You have probably already figured this one out if you are keeping tabs on what separates one Birth Order from the next. One's sense of humor is significant, because misunderstood communication can break down relationships. If someone cracks a joke and you take it as a personal insult—well, the whole world can change. Never joke about a woman's age!

Onlies tend to use sarcasm. Sarcasm changes the meaning of what people say by giving their words a twist. For example an Only Child might say, "Sure, you want to help me. You just want my money."

First Born humor is the kind that makes a person blush. Good First Born humor is pleasantly embarrassing, a comment followed by a smile that indicates humorousness. This may be an observation about a person's appearance, demeanor, or a surprising expression. Never scold Nancy!

Second Born humor is a teasing type of humor delivered with a mock seriousness that makes the recipient take a second look. It often has an element of suggesting improvement when a person has already done well.

Third Born humor usually contains an element of comparison that can be taken as a putdown. Good Third Born humor makes the comparison appear funny.

Some Fourth Borns likes to insult with their humor. A Fourth Born man walked up to his minister after a funeral, for example, and asked in a loud voice if the minister made a lot of money from funerals. Luckily for the Fourth Born, the minister recognized the fact that the man was trying to be funny and said, "No, I don't get enough of them," and the two men laughed. If the minister had not been aware of the dynamics of Birth Order Personality, he may have been offended. Instead, they both were able to enjoy a laugh.

Good Birth Order humor invites the other person to respond with their own brand of Birth Order humor. For example, a Fourth Born greeted his brother-in-law and his wife with Fourth Born humor by saying, "What's the matter? Couldn't you afford a motel so you had to come sponge off of us?" the way it was said, in mock seriousness, made it apparent it was humor. The brother-in-law responded with First Born humor by saying, "Calm down, you old coot. I'm here to see my sister, not you." They both laughed. Their friendship was affirmed.

If either had taken the other seriously, they could have been very offended. In fact, much conflict that people experience in relationships is misunderstood humor.

Why is humor negative? That's what makes it humor. Positive statements made to others are not funny. People are supposed to take them seriously. People are supposed to treat most negative statements as a joke. Of course, sometimes people are serious in their nasty remarks.

Each individual thinks and processes ideas and thoughts in a way that would make sense to others who share the same Birth Order Personality. Think about it. If, for example, you know a few First Borns, you could probably imagine them all asking the "What happens after we die?" question. It would fit with their general approach toward life.

Each Birth Order Personality also tends to process irrational thoughts in the same fashion. As always, this does not mean that you are going have the thoughts associated with your Personality, but you may know someone who has had them.

Only Child: "People can read minds; that's how they control me." This reflects the Only Child's affinity for the imaginary.

First Born: "People do not care about each other, so

there is no love for me." This reflects the First Born's lack of confidence in truly being loved. They complain too much.

Second Born: "Feelings don't matter, so I can do what is necessary." This arises from the Second Born's tendency to turn off his or her feelings. because it's rarely safe to talk.

Third Born: "Life can be made absolutely safe; so I have to protect or be protected." This stems from the Third Born's feelings of vulnerability.

Fourth Born: "Everything is done on purpose, so I can be angry." This reflects the Fourth Born's belief that since everyone else is mature, they do things intentionally; but since the Fourth Born is immature, he or she cannot be held accountable for his or her actions.

If each Birth Order has its own pattern of irrational thinking, it would also make sense that each one has its own reasons for being depressed. The following should give you additional insights into each Birth Order as well as some ideas of what can trigger depression.

Only Child

Major cause of depression: Chaos. Inability to put order into life.

Other causes: When others who matter feel depressed; when Onlies have too much to worry about and life seems to be all work and no play.

First Born

Major cause of depression: Being thought badly of by others. It does not seem to matter whether the opinions have a basis in fact or not.

Other causes: Guilt, failure, inability to impress others, being surpassed by others.

Second Born

Major cause of depression: Lack of caring by others. Second Borns tend to be sensitive to others paying attention to their feelings. "They don't care how their harsh words

Other causes: Bad relationships, burnout. and/or insults make me feel."

Third Born

Major cause of depression: Overwhelming fear. The fear does not relate to any realistic danger but to the fear of fear itself.

Other causes: Boredom, anxiety, being disappointing to others, inability to please someone.

Fourth Born

Major cause of depression: Anger at being trapped. The feeling of being trapped is psychological rather than based in reality, and may actually be relieved by being "trapped," as in prison.

Other causes: Being left out, losing a partner to someone else, being made to feel immature, regrets over things left undone, Fourth Born internal compulsion to sabotage own life.

And how about some advice about not taking advice? Here's some advice you should not take from each Birth Order.

- You should not take advice from Onlies on how to relate to people. Although Onlies love to give advice on how to relate to others, they themselves relate to others as if they were imaginary.
- You should not take advice from First Borns on predicting how people will behave. First Borns love to

give advice on which to expect from others, even though they themselves do not understand what motivates others.

- You should not take advice from Second Borns on how to express feelings. Second Borns will give advice on expressing feelings despite the fact they are struggling with expressing their own. *Because it's rarely safe to talk about being correct*
- You should not take advice from Third Borns on how to stand up for yourself. Although Third Borns love to give advice about standing up for yourself, they don't take this type of advice to heart themselves.
- You should not take advice from a Fourth Born on how to negotiate. Fourth Borns will give advice on negotiating when they themselves do not know how to use the power that is necessary for negotiation.

This isn't meant to be negative. Really. It's information so that you can understand and make decisions based on material that is fair and accurate. Now that you know how to spot bad advice according to Birth Order, you will be able to match wits with any Personality.

Want some more information? The next chapter will explore various ways in which to communicate and interact by using the Birth Order Personality knowledge you have gained from this book. This knowledge will increase the more you come to grasp this meaningful way to relate to yourself and the people in your life.

● ● ● ● ●

Knowledge itself is power.
—Francis Bacon

Chapter Fifteen

I Told You This Would Work: Using Birth Order in Everyday Life

Have you ever taken a cross-country car trip? Maybe you and the family once drove from St. Louis to California. Eventually, the kids started going crazy, you started going crazy, and before you knew it, all you cared about was getting there. You forgot about the side trips to see the canyons and rivers and lakes; you forgot about the journey. The destination was all you cared about.

Understanding Birth Order can help you to see how important the journey can be. You don't have to hurry through life, constantly worrying that you are never going to figure it out—or the people who share portions of your life. Birth Order can make the journey a wonderfully exciting and fulfilling experience.

As in every life, there will most likely be more than a few

bumps in the road, but understanding Birth Order can help smooth out the ride. If you knew there was a pothole in the road up ahead, wouldn't you drive around it? (Of course, Third Borns, those risk-taking creatures that they are, would probably just drive right over it and hope they wouldn't blow out a tire.)

A number of clients have told Cliff Isaacson that they got more out of the first session with him than they have in months of therapy with someone else. The use of Birth Order in counseling sessions accelerates the results of psychotherapy, accomplishing in hours what often takes months to accomplish with traditional forms of psychotherapy. In fact, 71 percent of Isaacson's clients come in for five sessions or less of counseling. Isaacson and his clients don't need lots of time to get where they need to go because they are driving on a paved road. Make sense?

Birth Order can also help pave the way for advances in psychotherapy. Just because we can get where we want to go faster with Birth Order does not mean that we'll spend less time on the road, so to speak; rather, with psychotherapy we will find more places to go.

Putting your new Birth Order knowledge into practice does not have to be a complicated ordeal. Always remember to enjoy the journey.

How about some ideas of positive things to say to each Birth Order Personality? Here are a few things you can use when circumstances are appropriate:

- "You handled yourself well in that situation." This is universally positive because Birth Order is a set of coping strategies. With this statement you are complimenting the coping abilities of any Personality.
- "You have a good sense of humor," or "That's funny." People always feel good when their humor is recognized. Also feel free to respond with your own type of humor.

See how simple this can be? The following positive comments have been adapted to the individual Birth Orders.
They can be used in a variety of situations and can really
set an upbeat tone.

For the Only Child

"You like to do things right, don't you?" This acknowledges the Only Child's efforts to do things properly.

"You organized that well." This recognizes the Only
Child's organizational skills.

"You deserve to be happy." This makes an Only Child
feel loved.

"You make me feel good." This connects with the Only
Child's desire to create happiness in others.

"You're so fair with everyone." This acknowledges the
Only Child's concept of justice.

For First Borns

"You did that well, but I like you because you are you."
This makes the First Born feel loved.

"That was impressive." The First Born welcomes admiration; it makes him or her feel good.

"You're a good leader," or "You took responsibility for
what was going on." This recognizes the First Born's natural
tendency to lead.

"You got a lot out of what was said." This shows you
appreciate the First Born's need to know what others think.

faithful is a better word - I would love to be appreciated for that - why does this statement feel like a putdown?

For Second Borns

"You are dependable." Acknowledging this characteristic
of Second Borns makes them feel appreciated.

"You saved us a lot of trouble when you found that," or

"You certainly pay attention to details." These statements highlight the value of the Second Born's attention to detail.

"Thank you for the helpful suggestions." This is a good statement to make when a Second Born has pointed out how you can do better—but you have to be sincere when you say it!

"You're sensitive to how others feel." This may not be apparent on the surface, but this is what Second Borns experience. Saying so will help you to connect with the Second Born.

—being told I'm selfish is a horrible putdown— don't ever say or imply that!

For Third Borns

"You certainly have creative ideas." A Third Born will enjoy having his or her ideas acknowledged.

"You are always there when someone needs you." This recognizes the Third Born's sense of compassion.

"You don't seem to be afraid of anything." The Third Born feels affirmed by this statement.

"I'm sorry life has been so difficult for you." Sympathy makes the Third Born feel loved, but don't wait for him or her to complain to say it.

"You make me feel safe." Being able to keep you from being afraid will make a Third Born happy.

For Fourth Borns

"You have done a lot of thinking about that, haven't you?" This is the supreme compliment for Fourth Borns, as they are used to feeling as if people reject their thinking.

"I like having you as part of our group." This makes the Fourth Born feel wanted, a very good feeling.

"You like to work hard, don't you?" Fourth Borns often take pride in their tendency to work hard.

"You make things easy for me." Fourth Borns like to know they make life easier for others.

"That must have been hard for you." This recognizes the Fourth Born's ability to handle difficult situations.

There are many ways to draw on what you know about someone's Birth Order to make him or her feel good. The above are suggestive of the kinds of things that can be said. As you gain a better understanding of each individual Birth Order, responding to each Personality in a positive way will become more and more natural.

Knowledge of Birth Order can help you to communicate with others on many different levels. Dan, for example, used it in the way he made his living. Dan, a Third Born, had just taken a new job selling adjustable beds. It was his responsibility to call on qualified leads developed by the company. Before he began selling Dan did some background research on Birth Order Personality so that he would know what to say to potential clients in order to make a sale.

Dan caught on to Birth Order Personality fairly quickly. He had some great ideas about how to approach each Birth Order. For example, Dan told Isaacson that when he was dealing with an Only Child, he would suggest that they deserve a good night's sleep, and he would say something like, "It is right to get this bed." He decided that it would make sense to let First Born clients read the letters written by satisfied users because First Borns like to know what others think, and that since Second Borns love details, he should let them read all of the product's specifications. Dan thought that it would be best to sympathize with the Third Borns' fear of buying an expensive item, and that Fourth Borns should be challenged with the difficulties involved in getting the bed, especially the financial aspects of the deal.

Dan would meet clients in their homes. Most of his clients had family photos, so Dan would break the ice by asking casual questions about the clients' families. (This also allowed him to establish the birth order of family members.)

He made his first sale to a Third Born who was tired
and never said a word during Dan's ninety-minute presentation. The man just sat with his elbows on the table and his
head propped up in his hands while his wife did all the
talking. At the end of the presentation Dan said to the man,
"It must be scary for you to put your name on the dotted
line and to commit yourself to spending this much money.
In fact, it must be scary for you to make this decision."

The man didn't say a word but turned to his wife and said,
"Emma, will you please pass the checkbook?" Way to go, Dan.

In three months Dan became the top salesperson in the
company. The average salesperson in this company was
selling to 30 percent of their contacts, while Dan was selling
to 70 percent. He was also making a lot of friends. People
invited him to come back to visit, they sent him letters, and
they called him. They liked Dan. His Birth Order–based
interventions did not feel like pressure to them, and they felt
as if Dan understood them and cared about them.

Interestingly enough, Dan's fellow salespeople attributed
his sales success to his personality and were never curious
about what he was doing.

See how fascinating this all is? Watch out the next time
you are shopping. Someone may have your Birth Order
pegged, and, before you know it, you'll be paying off new
charges on your VISA bill. The way you talk, your body language, your facial expressions, or your general appearance
may give you away.

Can you see how important Birth Order knowledge is to
communication? The following will help you to better understand how each Birth Order handles communicating.

Only Child Communication

Communication style: meta-communication. The Only
Child doesn't say exactly what he or she means, but

something close to it. For example, Onlies might say to a child, "It's time to go to bed," rather than, "I would like for you to go to bed now."

Listening: Projection. The Only Child will listen for confirmation of what he or she already thinks about the other person.

Reception: When the Only Child speaks, another Only Child will understand it, a First Born will believe what he or she says, the Second Born will evaluate it, the Third Born will provide an alternative idea, and the Fourth Born will either deny or accept it.

First Born Communication

Communication style: tentative. The First Born does not want to commit him- or herself to a position until he or she has discovered what you think.

Listening: A First Born tends to listen for opportunities to impress the other person.

Reception: While an Only Child will tend to be unimpressed with a First Born, another First Born will have trouble connecting with him or her, a Second Born will tend to criticize the First Born, a Third Born will appreciate the fact that the First Born seems receptive to ideas, and the Fourth Born will tend to find a First Born of little threat to him or her.

Second Born Communication

Communication Style: written. Second Borns prefer writing notes over communicating verbally so as to avoid emotion. Their communication tends to be evaluative, expressing judgment.

Listening: Tends to listen for errors, responding to them with correction or judgment.

Reception: An Only Child will tend to relate to a Second

Born well, the First Born will feel uneasy, a Second Born will resonate with another Second Born, the Third Born will shrug off what the Second Born says, and a Fourth Born will use logic against a Second Born.

Third Born Communication

Communication style: bottom line. Third Borns tend to jump to the conclusion rather than giving a lot of details.

Listening: They listen for what motivates the other person—wanting to please others—and for conclusions. They get bored with too much detail.

Reception: Onlies may be uncomfortable with the Third Born's lack of organization, a First Born may be mesmerized by a Third Born, the Second Born may find a Third Born frustrating, two Third Borns will move away from each other, and a Fourth Born may feel overpowered by a Third Born.

Fourth Born Communication

Communication style: introductions. Fourth Born communication starts with an introductory question or statement that may lead to more, depending on whether or not you have shown interest in what the Fourth Born has said. May use forceful means to get others to listen.

Listening: Tends to deny or accept what others say without evaluating.

Reception: The Only Child will often find a Fourth Born frustrating, First Borns will find themselves off balance with a Fourth Born, a Second Born will tend to go along with a Fourth Born, the Third Born can find a Fourth Born aggravating, and other Fourth Borns will tend to be passive with them.

• • • • •

These are not hard-and-fast rules, but general observations. Although you will find many exceptions to these observations, since so many more factors than Birth Order enter into communication, they can serve as a general guide and should help you gain some insight into communication styles.

> Two roads diverged in a wood, and I
> took the one less traveled by, and
> that has made all the difference.
> —Robert Frost

Chapter Sixteen

A World of Greater Understanding: The Future of Birth Order

Do you feel like a Birth Order Personality expert now? You could be. More important, are you having fun yet? The process of learning about Birth Order Personality and putting it to use in our daily lives should be fun. Since people will pursue what is fun, they will most likely increasingly begin to use their knowledge of Birth Order in their relationships. Let's hope so.

Once ideas about Birth Order begin circulating through word of mouth, these concepts will spread like wildfire. People will have to learn about Birth Order out of self-defense! But they will also have fun doing it. Forget about mind reading; Personality reading will be the next wave of the future.

Birth Order is going to make the world of relationships a fun place to be. These changes will be seen in the home, at work, at school, in the neighborhood, in the church—wherever people get together. In a way, Birth Order is going to turn the lights on in relationships. It may take some people a while to get used to the light, but eventually they'll find that their relationships will be much more candid than they are now and will be built on understanding rather than gut-level reactions.

This new level of understanding will have so many ramifications that it would be impossible to name them all. Just imagine a world in which people have a greater tolerance for others because they are able to understand how different people think and why they behave in certain ways.

Look for greater harmony in families, marriages, workplaces, schools, and communities. Of course, not all conflicts and misunderstandings will be eliminated, but it is possible that a general lessening of anger will become apparent in our societies. This prospect is especially important, given the escalating level of violence throughout the world.

Birth Order will also enable people to mount a greater challenge to those who are emotional bullies—like the four-year-old Fourth Born who was able to stop her older brother from teasing her by telling him, "You are such a First Born!" Birth Order will empower lots of people. Rude clerks, arrogant doctors, unreasonable teachers, and tyrannical employers will meet their match in people who understand Birth Order.

As more sources of problems are identified through the use of Birth Order, there will be changes in psychotherapy. The need for psychotherapy will be increased, however, as people recognize through Birth Order how numerous areas of their life could be improved.

Just as the speed of the automobile increased the amount of travel by allowing people to go more places, so Birth Order will increase the amount of psychotherapy by enabling more people to make changes faster. The subsequent need for more therapists will be met by the increasing numbers of students doing research on Birth Order.

Birth Order will cause people to give each other more feedback on their personalities—often whether they want it or not! This feedback will give rise to more personal change, however, because Birth Order enables a person to look at his or her own behavior in a detached way—as a function of Birth Order rather than as a part of who they are. When we are caught up in our Birth Order, we are helpless. When we are able to step outside of it, we gain power over it. This is what can happen across our society.

On the scary side, there will be no place to hide. It will be hard to put on a front when people are able to see through you because of Birth Order. In this sense, Birth Order pressures people to make changes they need to make. However, it is hoped that this will cause people to take more responsibility for themselves. This has positive ramifications for society worth thinking about.

Don't be surprised if there is a strong attempt to undermine the effectiveness of Birth Order. There is always a vested interest in maintaining the status quo. Many people do not like change because they find it frightening. It is often more comfortable to stay in one place than to expand and grow and change and learn.

There is also much invested in understanding human nature in traditional ways. People of the old school may fight those who are convinced of Birth Order's power. Birth Order will cause some wonder what do we do with all the training, all the materials, all the schemes of personality that are used to define human behavior to fit our current psychotherapy. When the automobile came, there were similar questions about what we would do with all the buggy manufacturers, the skilled buggy drivers, the harness makers, the livery stables, and the oat farmers. Of course, with the coming of the automobile came all kinds of benefits—which is exactly what will happen with Birth Order—we are going to be able to go farther faster and more efficiently.

Birth Order puts the understanding of human nature in the hands of average people rather than keeping it confined in the hands of the experts. Experts are still necessary, of course, but the knowledge must be shared. Birth Order is just in its infant stages, but it about to burst forth upon the world. Think of the possibilities, the potential—think mostly about a world where people understand each other.

Now get out there and have some fun with your own Birth Order and with the Birth Order challenges that await you and the people who are in your life.

The important thing is not
to stop questioning.
—Albert Einstein

Chapter Seventeen

Who, What, When, Where, and Why: The Most Frequently Asked Questions about Birth Order

1. What is Birth Order?
Birth Order is a set of five Personalities. For want of a better label, we call these Personalities by the position in which they are usually found in the family: Only Child, First Born, Second Born, Third Born and Fourth Born.

2. How does it differ from chronological birth order?
Most of the time Birth Order Personality correlates with the chronological birth order position. There are many exceptions, however, which can usually be explained by certain rules.

3. How was this concept discovered?
Cliff Isaacson discovered Birth Order Personality when he

compared the life mini-scripts as defined by Dr. Taibi Kahler with the personalities of his five children.

4. Why do I need to know my Birth Order?

The better you understand Birth Order Personality, the better you understand yourself and others. This, in turn, can do wonders for your emotional well-being and the quality of your relationships.

5. How can I determine my Birth Order?

Start with your chronological birth order. Your Birth Order Personality is likely to be the same as your chronological position. Then, using this book—including the Birth Order Assessment, the T-shirts, the Birth Order Inventory, and the Birth Order Matrix—compare your personality to the descriptions of each Birth Order Personality. If you are still confused, ask a friend who knows you well to go through the materials with you, as you may have trouble seeing yourself as you really are.

6. Can a person have more than one Birth Order Personality?

No, a person has only one Birth Order Personality and it is a coherent, distinct personality, not made up of bits and pieces of several Birth Order Personalities. A person can have secondary characteristics from two other Birth Order Personalities, however, and those will help determine how a person expresses his or her primary Personality.

7. Isn't this putting people in a box or giving them a label?

People are already living in psychological boxes that Cliff has identified through the discovery of Birth Order Personality. The label is necessary for communication. We do not impose labels on people, but on the Personality—being careful to discover what that Personality is before we label it.

8. Can someone adopt traits from another Personality?
It would be nice if we could, wouldn't it? Or at least it might
seem that way. Our Personalities are quite stable, however,
not changeable. What we can do is *adapt* the ways we use
our Personality traits rather than trying to adopt new traits.
Specifically, we can choose careers, hobbies, recreation, education, and even life partners that enable us to make the best
use of them.

**9. Is it possible to keep some Birth Order Personality
traits and throw away others, or are we stuck with the
whole package?**
We cannot throw away any Birth Order Personality traits;
they're ours for life. However, we must not confuse the
problems associated with each Birth Order Personality with
traits with which we are stuck. For example, the feelings of
being smothered, and of guilt, inadequacy, vulnerability, and
anger associated with the Birth Order Personalities do not
have to be retained. They are problems that can be solved.
Also, we need to be aware not to use the phrase, "I can't
help it; that's my Birth Order," except in humor, because
doing so puts us in the victim role emotionally. Birth Order
knowledge is meant to empower us, not to place us in
victim roles.

**10. Do some people have "stronger" Birth Order
Personalities than others?**
Yes. Birth Order Personalities are developed as coping
strategies early in life. If family life is harmonious, coping
is not needed to the extent that it is in a dysfunctional
family, making Birth Order less dominant. The more a child
has to cope with, the stronger the Birth Order Personality
will be throughout life—or until one learns from *The Birth
Order Effect*.

11. Can a person change his or her Birth Order Personality?

Nope. It's been tried, but it hasn't worked. Doing so would involve going back to change the early experiences that formed the original Birth Order Personality. It is better to enjoy the Birth Order Personality you have; after all, you're familiar with it, it works for you, and you have learned a lot in using it. Creating another Birth Order Personality might mean starting life all over again. Would you want to go back to the crib?

12. Is it possible to make a mistake when determining a person's Birth Order?

Yes. The person coming from a happy home may have a Personality that is very hard to diagnose (see question 10). Quite often, having a good relationship with one's parents can cause a person's secondary Birth Order Personality characteristics, which come from one's parents, to be more apparent than his or her primary Personality traits. Also, when people are in social situations in which they are comfortable, their Birth Order Personality may become hidden behind secondary characteristics. The true primary Birth Order Personality comes out when an individual is under stress, which is when misdiagnoses become apparent.

13. What is the purpose of knowing your Birth Order?

Knowing your own Birth Order means you know yourself. In knowing yourself, you can look at yourself from the outside; i.e., you can dissociate from yourself. This dissociation allows you to be objective about yourself, to accept yourself, and to make changes that you want to make. It allows you to stop making demands on yourself that you cannot meet. For example, if you are an Only Child with a Third Born mother, you like to be organized and aware of what's going on at all times, while she is relaxed and likes to "go with the flow." Being aware of your differences will make it okay for the two of you to do things your own way. You can organize for your-self, while she will be free to fly by the seat of her pants. You are not wrong, and she is not wrong, it's just that you have different Birth Order Personalities.

14. Can several children in a family all have the same Birth Order?

Yes, but they each would be an Only Child; in fact, one family of six Only Children comes to mind. Once you have a First Born, the next will be a Second Born, and the fol-lowing a Third Born. Siblings cannot all be First Borns, Second Borns, Third Borns or Fourth Borns. But they can all be Onlies if Grandmother came in for a few days after each child was born.

15. When is it best to determine your Birth Order?

There is no particular age at which it is best to determine your Birth Order, but even young children can identify with their Birth Order. One young Fourth Born we know loves being a Fourth Born, finds her identity in it, and feels like she can be herself rather than like one of her older siblings or even her mother. She is her own person with her own Personality and her own behaviors. She likes herself. She's only four years old.

16. Is it possible to predict a person's behavior by his or her Birth Order?

We can predict behavior by Birth Order in a general way. We can predict that a person might be happy in a particular career, for example, based on Birth Order. However, pre-dicting individual behaviors based on Birth Order is tricky, because life experiences and perceptions based on them affect what people choose. It is much easier to analyze behavior after the fact through Birth Order Personality.

Birth Order Personalities do, however, have an instinctual feel for how Birth Order Personalities ahead of them will behave. Fourth Borns, for example, tend to be able to tell what First, Second, Third, and other Fourth Borns will do. First Borns only know what other First Borns will do, and that only vaguely. No Birth Order can predict Only Child behavior instinctually except for another Only Child. Also, Onlies cannot predict any other Personality's behavior, although they think they can.

17. What are some good reasons for me to know and understand my Birth Order?

- It allows you to organize your life according to your strengths. Each Birth Order Personality has its own particular strengths, and going with your strong points can make your life more productive and more enjoyable.
- It enables you to relate to others as an equal—to stop using your differences from others as a reason for either putting yourself down or holding yourself as being superior to them. It allows you to relate as an equal to people who think, feel, and act differently from the way you do.
- It enables you to avoid the pitfalls that await those who ignore their weaknesses. You can eliminate much stress in your life when you recognize how your Birth Order helps to determine what those stressors are.
- It enables you to overcome your fear of being vulnerable because of other people's difference from you. Understanding others allows you to feel confident in dealing with them.
- It enables you to feel connected to the world rather than feeling estranged because of your difference from others. You can feel as if you belong—especially knowing that others share your Personality.

18. Can knowing my Birth Order help me in my marriage?
Definitely! Birth Order Personality differences that are not
recognized or understood can create much conflict in marriages. Those spouses who are informed about each other's
Birth Order Personality find that they can not only accept
each other's differences, but enjoy them. These differences
often become a source of good-natured humor rather then
aggravation.

19. Can Birth Order help me as a parent?
Yes. Birth Order will benefit your children by helping you
to treat each child individually according to his or her
Personality rather than trying to put each child in a box
that fits your concept of personality. This will help you
avoid making the error of comparing your children to each
other and will allow your children to be themselves. It
makes children happier when they feel as if they are
understood, and that will, in turn, make your life as a
parent much happier. You can avoid making the error of
comparing your children to each other and allows your
children to be themselves.

**20. Can knowing about Birth Order help me in the work-
place?**
Knowing your Birth Order can help you in the following
career-related ways:

- It will assist you in choosing the kind of work you
  would be happiest doing over the long haul. For
  example, if you are a Third Born you would probably
  enjoy sales; if you are a Second Born you would
  probably like accounting. A Third Born accountant or
  a Second Born salesperson would most likely find his
  or her work to be stressful.
- It can enable you to better interact with your
  coworkers because you will better understand their

ways. It will also help you in responding to workplace humor. Some of this humor can be very cutting, but understanding Birth Order Personality will equip you to understand it and deal with it.

- It can help you understand how and why your supervisors express themselves the way they do. It will give you insight into their expectations and how to satisfy them. It will also help you to accept their way of giving orders—which might otherwise anger you if you had no knowledge of their Personality.

- It will give you insight into the most common cause of management failure in companies: the *"Titanic* effect" caused by a Second Born in charge. When a critical Second Born who's feeling inadequate, becomes a CEO, the effect on a business can be as destructive as the iceberg was to the *Titanic.* Recognizing this, you may want to get off the *Titanic*—or out of that business or industry before you suffer personally. On the other hand, if you are a Second Born who has been put in charge, this knowledge can help you take special pains to think about the feelings of the people who work for the company, how a company prospers when the employees support it, and how employees support a company when they believe the company cares about them.

- It will aid you in deciding whether or not to accept a promotion. For example, if you are a successful Third Born salesperson, your company may be tempted to promote you to sales manager, reasoning that you can inspire the other sales personnel to do well. Yet what usually happens when a top salesperson is made manager, is that the company loses a good salesperson and gains a mediocre manager. In this case, then, you might want to continue doing what you love to do—sell—and leave the management to someone else. If you were the one hiring the sales manager, on the other hand, you might want to choose a people-oriented Fourth Born, who would make a wonderful manager—even if he or she is not a top salesperson.

21. Does Birth Order just focus on negatives?

Each Birth Order Personality has its strengths as well as its weaknesses. For effectiveness, it is best to try and build on the strengths and deal with the weaknesses.

22. What is the greatest thing that can be said about Birth Order?

It takes the knowledge of human nature out of the hands of experts and puts it into the hands of ordinary people. Many tests provide psychological information, but you need to be qualified by education or a license to use it. Birth Order knowledge offers even more psychological information than many of these tests and is accessible to the average person.

23. What about people who say this is just another goofy fad?

Those who say that have not really explored the concept—or *The Birth Order Effect*. Psychological professionals who call it a fad are most likely immersed in another kind of psychotherapy that they feel the need to protect.

24. How can Birth Order help me?

The extent to which Birth Order can help you completely depends upon how much you make of it. You can engage with it superficially or in depth. People have used it to enhance their careers, nurture their relationships, and improve their emotional health. Some people take away only what they need to solve a particular problem or achieve a particular goal, while others use it in every way they can. The choice is yours.

25. Why has it taken so long for someone to discover this type of Birth Order?

A number of factors produced the conditions that allowed Cliff Isaacson to discover Birth Order Personality, including the training in Transactional Analysis that acquainted him with the five mini-scripts; his curiosity about Birth Order; and the fact that he had five children with whom to compare the mini-scripts. The combination of his First Born Personality Birth Order traits with his Only Child and Third Born secondary characteristics furthered his goal of understanding Birth Order Personality by leading him to organize what he discovered and make comparisons so as to pinpoint patterns. In addition, Isaacson was a pastor unencumbered by psychological presuppositions but who had the opportunity to work with lots of people in his counseling sessions. In a sense, he discovered Birth Order Personality accidentally, and he feels privileged to have done it.

26. What about the old ideas of the first-born being a leader—and where is the middle child in Birth Order?

The First Born Personality is a leader, but not a manager—a distinction not made in the old Adlerian ideas of birth order. No one has been able to define the middle child personality because, in reality, the middle child can be any of the five Birth Order Personalities. All that people have been able to do is define the middle child in general terms based on suppositions that do not by any means apply to all middle children.

27. Is there more to discover about Birth Order Personality?

Yes. Hundreds of students are already doing various projects on Birth Order, from science fair projects to master's theses. Many people are currently being introduced to Birth Order via Isaacson's Web site, *www.birthorderplus.com.*

28. Does Cliff Isaacson always use Birth Order in his counseling services?

Always. He tries to establish the Birth Order Personality of the client in the first few minutes of the initial session; otherwise, he would be working in the dark. A person's problem itself is not enough of a clue to his or her Personality because the nature of the problem depends on the Birth Order Personality. For example, though a Third Born and an Only Child may both report feeling anxious, a Third Born's anxiety tends to spring from a feeling of vulnerability, while an Only Child's anxiety usually stems from worry about what is going to happen.

29. Why is this such an effective way of helping people?

There are several reasons:

- Establishing a client's Birth Order Personality information—and sharing with the client immediately—gives him or her a feeling of being understood. One man reported that he had only gone for counseling because his wife had wanted him to do so, and without any real expectation that it would do anything for him. He said Isaacson told him so much about himself in the first twenty minutes, however, that he was convinced this was no ordinary counseling session. He's since come back for many sessions on his own without any outside pressure.

- Providing clients with an understanding of their Birth Order Personality enables them to look closely at their behavior, feelings and thought patterns without having to be defensive. So many people are afraid that they need counseling because something is wrong with them. It is a great relief for them to know that they are only living Birth Order patterns that others are also experiencing.

- Using Birth Order understanding helps to very quickly identify the nature of the problem the person is experiencing. Effective therapy starts in the first session, so the client leaves feeling better, having learned some things and been given a sense of hope that things will improve. As a result, they are usually eager to come back for another session. Isaacson has had clients who initially came in fearfully, lest someone they knew see them, who, after three sessions, began freely sharing with others the information that they had been for counseling.
- Understanding Birth Order empowers the client. Isaacson has had many clients who, in turn, were able to help others with what they have learned in their own counseling sessions. Isaacson operates on the notion that the client has a right to know what the therapist knows, so therapeutic information is shared freely.
- Birth Order can make counseling fun for clients in that they learn how to laugh at the ways in which they act out their Birth Orders. Isaacson spends some time laughing with most of his clients before their counseling is done. They leave his center with a smile on their face.
- Changes made as a result of learning about Birth Order are permanent, and more changes become possible as the client continues to ponder what he or she has learned. Isaacson has been told by former clients of changes they were able to make years after their final session.

30. Does one Birth Order–related success story stand out?
There are so many success stories it is difficult to single out just one. However, one dramatic story concerns a man whose doctor sent him for counseling because he was depressed. The man had had a stroke and could not

converse; about all he could say coherently were yes or no. His wife was of minimal assistance in interpreting what he said. However, because Isaacson knew that the man was a Second Born, and that at the root of his depression was the Second Born's characteristic feeling of inadequacy, which had been exacerbated by the stroke-induced disability, Isaacson was able to help him overcome his depression without needing much feedback from him other than a yes or no. It took only a few sessions to accomplish what would have been impossible had Isaacson needed to obtain lots of information from the man.

31. Is there a Web site that has more information about Birth Order?
Yes, *www.birthorderplus.com.*

32. Does Cliff Isaacson ever give workshops on Birth Order?
Yes, he has taught numerous workshops on Birth Order through many colleges. He has also spoken on Birth Order to groups throughout the country and plans to continue doing so.

33. Are more books planned on the subject of Birth Order Personality?
Yes. Isaacson intends to write a number of related books, including those that focus specifically on marriage and parenting.

34. What would the world be like if everyone understood Birth Order Personality?
If everyone knew about Birth Order, they would view themselves in a new light and would find it easier to deal with their own personality issues. They would also relate to others differently, because they would understand them better. The world would most likely be a much more forgiving and compassionate place.

Index

A

accomplishments, 80–81
Adler, Alfred, 7–8
admiration, 81–84, 163–64
adversity
  and marriage, 171–72
  and Onlies, 66–67, 193, 194
  and strength of Birth Order
    characteristics, 34, 43,
    159–60, 171–72, 221
advice, 55–56, 202–3
age, 35, 39–40
agreement, 81–82, 84, 87–88
analytical thinkers, 136–37, 140
anger, 113, 126, 141–42
anxiety, 114–15
appearance, physical, 99
approval, 81–84, 163–64

artistic talent, 103
authority, 103

B

behavior, 8–9, 223–24
Berne, Eric, 5
Birth Order Matrix, 25–32
Birth Order Personalities,
  39–43
  adapting to, 221
  advantages of knowing,
    220, 222–23, 224
  age set by, 39–40
  development of
    characteristics, 35–39,
    160
  early awareness of, 35, 223

Parents—*continued*
  See also secondary
    characteristics
peacemaking traits, 91, 103,
  192
perfectionism, 89, 95–96, 98,
  100–101, 113
privacy, 55
professions. *See* workplace
psychotherapy, 206, 216
putdown humor, 199

R
respect, 81–84, 163–64
role models, 187–88
rules, 102

S
salespeople, xi, 114, 123,
  209–10
sarcasm, 199
schedules, 61–63
secondary characteristics,
  147–58, 220
  chart, 151
  and determining Birth
    Order Personalities,
    222
  effects on daughters,
    153–55
  effects on sons, 156–58
  of Onlies, 66, 150
  rules of, 148–58
  and spouse selection, 150,
    172–75, 177–84
  See also parents

Second Born Birth Order
  Personalities, 6, 89–104
  advice from, 203
  and authority, 103
  causes of depression in,
    202
  characteristics, 46, 90–95,
    100–104
  communicating with, 165,
    207–8, 211–12
  competitiveness of, 94–95,
    97
  and criticism, 96–97, 98,
    99, 134, 164–65
  feelings of inadequacy,
    94–100, 107–8
  importance of physical
    appearance to, 99
  irrational thoughts of, 201
  and marriage, 178–79,
    181–82
  neatness of, 93–94
  needs as children, 191
  organizational skills of, 100
  as parents, 189, 192–93
  peacemaking traits of, 91,
    103, 192
  perfectionism of, 89, 95–96,
    98, 100–101, 113
  relationships with First
    Borns, 164
  relationships with Third
    Borns, 109–10, 165
  and rules, 102
  self-discipline, 103
  sense of humor, 199
  suppression of emotions,
    97–99

trust in experts, 100
use of logic, 97–98
in the workplace, 101
self-discipline, 103
self-help authors, 55–56
self-knowledge, 132–38,
144–45
siblings, 34–38
First Borns, 72–74, 76
Fourth Borns, 41, 134–35,
143–44
influence on Birth Order
Personalities, 41–42
and loss of love, 40,
42–43, 74, 76
Onlies, 35–36, 223
Second Borns, 109–10, 164,
165
Third Borns, 109–10,
127–28, 130, 165
Smith, Edward John, 100
social gatherings, 143
sons, 156–58
Spears, Britney, 103
speeds, 60
stressful situations, 148, 149,
150

T

teasing sense of humor, 199
temper tantrums, 65
tests for Birth Order
Personalities, 16–24
Third Born Birth Order
Personalities, 6, 105–23
accommodating nature of,
165–66

advice from, 203
and anger, 113
and boredom, 117–19
causes of depression in,
202
characteristics, 46, 106–9,
115–23
communicating with, 208,
212
compassion of, 121–22
creation of anxiety by,
114–15
creativity of, 122–23
entrepreneurial traits of,
153
and fear, 107, 111–13, 116,
120
hostility of, 115
inclination toward
comparison, 123
and interruptions, 119
irrational thoughts of, 201
and loneliness, 118–19
and marriage, 179–80,
183–84
need for changes, 118
needs as children, 191,
194–95
as parents, 41–42, 189
perfectionism in, 113
relationships with others,
109–10, 115–16, 121–23,
127–28, 130, 165
sense of humor, 199
suppression of emotions,
117
vulnerability of, 107–17,
119–21, 127–28, 130